T0286992

Also by Douglas MacKinnon

The Dawn of a Nazi Moon: Book One

Liberty Lessons
From Those Who Risked *All* to Sign
𝕿𝖍𝖊 𝕯𝖊𝖈𝖑𝖆𝖗𝖆𝖙𝖎𝖔𝖓 𝖔𝖋 𝕴𝖓𝖉𝖊𝖕𝖊𝖓𝖉𝖊𝖓𝖈𝖊

BEFORE *they* and the
4th of July are BANNED

𝕯𝖔𝖚𝖌𝖑𝖆𝖘 𝕸𝖆𝖈𝕶𝖎𝖓𝖓𝖔𝖓

A POST HILL PRESS BOOK
ISBN: 978-1-63758-424-8
ISBN (eBook): 978-1-63758-425-5

The 56:
Liberty Lessons From Those Who Risked All to Sign
The Declaration of Independence
© 2022 by Douglas MacKinnon
All Rights Reserved

Cover Design by Cody Corcoran

Post Hill Press
New York • Nashville
posthillpress.com

Published in the United States of America
2 3 4 5 6 7 8 9 10

For today's Patriots *seeking to keep the memories of our* **Founding Fathers** *burning bright and the Republic they created strong, free, fair, and forever alive.*

"I have never had a feeling politically that did not spring from the sentiments embodied in the *Declaration of Independence*."

—President Abraham Lincoln, Independence Hall, Philadelphia, Pennsylvania, February 22, 1861

CONTENTS

Part One

"THOSE WHO FAIL TO LEARN FROM
HISTORY ARE DOOMED TO REPEAT IT"

INTRODUCTION

The overriding and desperate need for a book such as this—at least in my mind—was given birth—ironically and hopefully fittingly—on the *4th of July, 2020*.

It was on that day, while doing research in preparation for writing a column heralding the increasingly critical importance of the 4th of July, I came across example after example after example of many on the Left not only denigrating our most sacred *American* holiday but also some actually calling for its very banning.

The ferocity of their comments and the deep and growing rage some of them seemed to exhibit froze me in place as I honestly wondered how so many—almost *all* standing atop platforms of wealth, privilege, political power, or all combined—had come to so hate the symbolic date of 𝕵𝖚𝖑𝖞 4, 1776, or…its celebration? A date that did give birth to a Republic that did *make possible* their tremendous wealth, privilege, political power, and…rage.

My very next thought literally sent a chill down my spine.

"What if they are not only successful in banning the 𝟦𝖙𝖍 𝖔𝖋 𝕵𝖚𝖑𝖞 but also, ultimately, in erasing the sacrifices, accomplishments, and very names of those who signed the Declaration of Independence on that fateful day?"

To those who believe such totalitarian censorship will never come to be in the United States of America, I would urgently ask them to review how quickly and brutally many on the Left not only were able to create the woke cancel culture but also use it to silence those they opposed and, in many cases, literally destroy their livelihoods and, consequently, their very lives in the process.

Will the day, which represents the act of those 56 men coming together as one to declare our independence from tyranny and our right to exist as a sovereign nation and a free people soon be altered, smeared, or outright "canceled?"

Flash ahead approximately 246 years from that historic and sacred time period, and the answer seems *quite obvious.* More and more of those in positions of great power and influence from the Left—who have come to dominate the media, academia, entertainment, science, and medicine—often via *discrimination* against Republicans, conservatives, or people of traditional faith—will most certainly try.

The fact that the Left now does control those major megaphones of our very nation certainly does tip the scales of monolithic-groupthink injustice strongly in their favor. Who is really left to stop them?

As that menacing cloud of total censorship moves closer and closer to a history many of us revere, one fact is already a reality. The meaning of the 4th of July and the celebration *of* the 4th of July have *already* been deliberately watered down by many on the Left over the last number of years.

It is clearly their hope that, as they do continue to water it down and it becomes lighter and lighter on the already revisionist pages of our *faux–American history* books, it will simply fade into nothingness to the current and future generations of Americans.

Disappear... forever.

To deny they are succeeding with this plan is to deny the very truth playing out before our eyes.

How can we stop it?

Unfortunately, looking toward the "leaders" from the "right" for support, comfort, and protection over the last couple of decades has proven to be a mixed bag at best and crushingly disheartening at worst.

Because the Left has come to so completely dominate the media, academia, entertainment, and—as we have witnessed these last few years—science, and medicine as well, many in positions of power from the Right have simply chosen to surrender to the massive and unchecked power of the Left. Not so shockingly, some from the Right have quite sadly and eagerly swept in the monetary crumbs they are fed by those who are slowly but surely subjugating what was once the United States of America.

In reality, the *only way out* of this assault upon the freedoms and liberties handed down to us by the 𝕱𝖔𝖚𝖓𝖉𝖎𝖓𝖌 𝕱𝖆𝖙𝖍𝖊𝖗𝖘 would be for those from the Right with the means ($) and power to do so, to get out of the peanut gallery of the arena that represents our nation and jump down to the dirty and uncertain floor of *that arena* to fight for their—and *our*—survival.

No one expressed this sentiment—or key ingredient for survival—better than Teddy Roosevelt when, on April 23, 1910, in Paris, he gave his now famous speech titled "Citizenship in a Republic." A speech now better known the world over simply as the "Man in the Arena."

Stressed the former president, in part:

> It is not the critic who counts; not the man who
> points out how the strong man stumbles, or
> where the doer of deeds could have done them
> better. The credit belongs to the man who is
> actually in the arena, whose face is marred by
> dust and sweat and blood; who strives val-
> iantly; who errs, who comes short again and
> again, because there is no effort without error
> and shortcoming; but who does actually strive
> to do the deeds; who knows great enthusiasms,
> the great devotions; who spends himself in a
> worthy cause; who at the best knows in the end
> the triumph of high achievement, and who at
> the worst, if he fails, at least fails while daring
> greatly, so that his place shall never be with
> those cold and timid souls who neither know
> victory nor defeat.[1]

For far too many years now, there have been voices out
there pretending to speak for the rights of Republicans, conservatives, libertarians, and people of traditional faith who
have continually, happily, and *quite profitably* placed themselves
within the camp of "those cold and timid souls who neither
know victory nor defeat."

It is not difficult at all to identify them. Most can now see
them for who and what they have become but choose to deny
the obvious out of a false sense of hope.

"Fool me once; shame on you. Fool me twice; shame on me."

Fool me three times, and...we may need a new country.

Unfortunately, it seems some within our nation have a bottomless capacity to be fooled by those willingly appeasing the Left in return for their meager crumbs.

Whether someone is spiritual or not, the truism "*The Lord helps those who help themselves*" applies in every single walk of life. Most especially when it comes to fighting for our rights and our liberty.

The fact is, that within our nation, there are Republicans, conservatives, and people of traditional faith who collectively are worth over $1 trillion. That's trillion with a "t." As in over one thousand *billion dollars*.

And yet, as a group, most choose to remain in the stands in the section housing "those cold and timid souls who neither know victory nor defeat."

These men and women could *instantly* make a massive difference if they but chose to jump into the arena to join the rapidly dwindling "souls" fighting for our rights and our very liberty.

How? Simply by investing in and creating their own megaphones of power.

Not, by the way, to turn them into "conservative" propaganda echo-chambers or rags. That would be just as wrong and just as vile as what the Left is now doing. But rather, to create honest and truthful sites and institutions where all people are welcome and all thoughts are allowed to be expressed without fear of reprisal or cancellation.

If they did choose to create their own media sites, their own colleges and universities, their own entertainment platforms, and their own social media outlets, and to start their own schools of medicine and science free of any and all politics and ideological indoctrination, *then* we would see a tremendous shift in the power and a true light of hope at the end of this very dark tunnel we now find ourselves existing within.

Tragically, there is no real evidence of that happening.

The cold, hard truth those of us who do believe in the dream of the Republic the Founding Fathers handed down to us and who do believe in equality for all, the rule of law, sovereign and protected borders, and a much less intrusive government is: For the most part...*we are leaderless and on our own.*

Period.

However, should we so choose, each of us can *individually* still be a keeper of that flame of liberty.

As the questions ask: "If not us, *who?* If not now, *when?*"

Each of us can still instill the lessons of liberty handed down from those who did put everything dear to them—most especially, their lives, the lives of their families, and all of their worldly possessions—on the line to sign the Declaration of Independence.

Like so many problems a nation encounters, the solution rarely can be found in the "macro" sense. As we have all learned—often at great expense to those in need—almost nothing ever gets solved at the macro or governmental level.

Take poverty and hunger for instance.

While over the last century of our nation, collectively tens of thousands of truly reprehensible people have personally enriched themselves off various "snake oil" solutions to poverty and hunger. And yet...here we still are. Millions of Americans at or below the poverty line. Hundreds of thousands of American children are dealing with "food insecurity" every single day of their lives.

I speak of this particular subject as one who knows it well. I grew up in abject poverty and was homeless often as a child.

By the time I had reached seventeen years of age, I and my family had been evicted from thirty-four homes. Living in cars while enduring relentless hunger and poverty have never been an academic exercise to me.

For years, that reality dictated my daily fight for survival.

For that reason—and many more—I learned the hard way that government handouts were not the solution. They were, in fact, ultimately part of the never-ending problem.

They were the problem because oftentimes they gave the poor barely enough to exist. Period. I learned that to break the bonds of poverty, I had to fight for my own survival, work as hard as I could, get as much education as possible, and accept personal responsibility for my actions.

I also came to realize as a young child that hunger and poverty could never be solved at the macro level. First and foremost, because of the endemic corruption connected with so many of the government programs or "charities" pretending to tackle the issues.

But…what I also came to realize at a very young age was that it *was possible* to make truly positive differences to hunger and poverty at the micro level.

And the nongovernmental, noncharity way was quite simple.

In our lives, we all know *someone* going through financial tough times, which bring about the poverty and hunger issues among us.

Be it a family member, a neighbor, a work colleague, or even a stranger we have come in contact with, we all know someone who—through no fault of their own—is being dragged down by the brutal realities of life.

Because of that, if each of us simply picks *one fellow human being* to help, we can effect a more positive change in poverty and hunger than all the corrupt and continually failing governmental and charity programs out there.

I mention all that because that *exact same philosophy* and *formula* applies to keeping the Torch of Liberty lit for not only us and our families but also for the Americans who will come after us.

Each one of us can pass along the core principles of freedom and individual liberty as articulated by the signers of the Declaration of Independence in 1776 to at least *one other American*. Be that American a child, a relative, a neighbor, or a work colleague.

Unless and until they imprison us or take our lives, they can't silence our individual voices. They can't stop us from individually passing along the truth.

With that in mind, and with the belief that nothing ever really gets solved at the macro level, I decided *now* is the time to use *my* voice and the platform I have to remember and honor The 56 who did come together as one to sign the Declaration of Independence.

I truly have come to believe that it's critically important to have a recent work in existence *that does speak* to their heroism, their patriotism, their foresight, their intelligence, and their courage.

What's the rush, you may ask?

Well, at this moment in time, I am blessed to have a publisher who not only believes in me but who also believes in publishing *all voices* and all viewpoints. But that moment in time may be fleeting at best, because almost the entirety of established "mainstream" publishing is controlled by the

Left or Far Left, with well over 90 percent of the staffs also leaning left.

Again, while many on the Left proclaim their "hate" of discrimination, no one uses it more effectively than them to gain control of those megaphones or industries and then work to *silence* the voices they oppose.

Precisely because of the growing "cancel culture" of the Left, the few publishers or imprints still in existence that do dare to publish all voices—including conservative, libertarian, or faith-based voices—are quickly coming under increased, sustained, and often slanderous attack. Most especially, from some of the Far Left staff *within* those very publishing houses.

One by one, outlets that do believe in amplifying the voices of any and *all* Americans—even if they are pragmatic, conservative, or faith-based—are either falling to this relentless assault or bending to the will and the dictates of the Left simply to stay in business so they can pay their bills and feed their families.

That deliberate silencing of the human voice, with few willing to speak out in defense of that most basic of human rights, brings to mind arguably the most powerful and chilling message with regard to that dangerous aggression.

As highlighted by the United States Holocaust Memorial Museum, Martin Niemöller (1892–1984) was a prominent Lutheran pastor in Germany. He emerged as an outspoken public foe of Adolf Hitler and spent the last seven years of Nazi rule in concentration camps.

Pastor Niemöller is best known for a lecture in which he stressed:

First they came for the socialists, and I did not speak out—because I was not a socialist.

Then they came for the trade unionists, and I did not speak out—because I was not a trade unionist.

Then they came for the Jews, and I did not speak out—because I was not a Jew.

Then they came for me—and there was no one left to speak for me.[2]

Now, some may think that referencing that disquieting passage is excessive when speaking of the United States of today. But is it really? After all, that was *the sole intent* of Pastor Niemöller. To leave those words behind as a warning to those who would come after him.

The *Merriam-Webster Dictionary* defines groupthink as "a pattern of thought characterized by self-deception, forced manufacture of consent, and conformity to group values and ethics."

The key words in that very accurate definition are "*self-deception*" and "*forced manufacture of consent.*"

Looking the other way because the trouble is not yet impacting us, is not only—as Pastor Niemöller articulated—a tragic part of human nature, but it is also something that always happens organically and seemingly, very slowly. Until, one day you wake up and *your* very world has changed for the worse.

Again, and I can't stress this enough, groupthink by *any-one*—be they conservative, liberal, Marxist, or faith-based—to create forced domination over fellow citizens for ideological, religious, or personal reasons is not only abhorrent but also truly dangerous. A tragic outcome *honest history* has taught us time and again.

That reality stressed, at *this* very moment in time, there are in fact power centers of the Left *forcefully* trying to censor, silence, and cancel voices and *books* they deem to be offensive to *their* current worldview.

Again, falling back upon Pastor Niemöller's warning, almost none of the leaders of the "liberal" publishing world—who control over 90 percent of the market—are speaking out *in defense* of the "conservative" publishers or imprints now under attack from the Left and their own liberal staff.

But...how long before the cancel culture mob decides that these "liberal" publishers *are themselves* now not quite "pure" enough when it comes to bowing before the dogma they are demanding to be obeyed? Who then, will speak up *for them* when *all are gone*?

That very question and new-world predicament is why I am in such a rush to get out a book speaking to the honor, courage, patriotism, and true genius of The 56 who signed the Declaration of Independence.

How long before *every platform* to get the word out may be taken from us?

↬

Speaking specifically about these 56 Signers, were they perfect or without flaws? Of course not. Far from it in some cases.

As human beings, we are *all* fallible. We have *all* made mistakes. We have *all* sinned. We *all* have regrets.

The **56 Signers** who created and validated the **Declaration of Independence** were flawed human beings. And yet, almost all were trying to do the very best they could under extremely trying conditions. As honest history has taught us in the past, many of these men lost so very much *precisely because* they did attach their name to that greatest of our founding documents.

Some on the Left have chosen to *only* view, judge, and attack these men by looking at their lives through an ideologically filtered prism of *today*. Not only is that wrong, but it can and does create a false narrative.

That, unfortunately, is exactly the point for some on the Left, whose *sole mission* is to vilify, invalidate, and ultimately cancel the names of these true American Patriots.

Should some out there not believe this, they need to merely look at the actions from *liberal to far left* faculty and students at institutions of higher learning such as Harvard, William & Mary, and the University of Virginia—to name but a few— who are seeking to defame and erase the names of some of the **Founding Fathers** associated with their schools. A trend which is only *accelerating* as I write this.

This point brings us to some of the irreversibly compromised "historians" now doing the bidding for the Left on a regular basis.

Precisely because of that extreme bias—which has been in existence for a few decades now—I came to believe that the *only way* to properly research the lives, sacrifices, and accomplishments of these **56 Signers** was to *go as far back in time* as possible. I came to realize that much of what had been written about these heroic men post-1970—and most especially post-2000—was often suspect at best and deliberately deceiving at worst. For it was about then, when many liberal faculty and leadership at American colleges and universities began their campaign to push out any faculty or voices from campus that countered their groupthink ideological narrative.

So, the farther back one could get into looking into these remarkable lives, the better chance their "history" was not written through the deliberately false lens of a liberal prism seeking to find and grossly exaggerate any perceived flaw—often *entirely* out of context—from that time that could be used to paint them with the broadest of prejudged brushes today.

Many on the Left who now seek to besmirch and ultimately cancel our **Founding Fathers** have absolutely *no idea* what was in their hearts and their souls during their truly heroic lifetimes. Nor do they care.

Again, their only goal is to ignorantly generalize and slander from atop their very own platforms of privilege via the cloudy and ideologically twisted prisms of today.

For example, as we have come to see with increasing frequency, one of the main and constant targets of some on the Left for the last couple of decades has been **Thomas Jefferson**.

There is nothing more abominable or obscene in the history of our Republic than slavery. Nothing.

It is a shame that will forever stain our history. Just as it is a shame and obscenity that will forever stain the history of almost every nation or society that ever existed on Earth. And it is a shame that, quite tragically, still goes on today in certain parts of our world.

Curiously—and also quite tellingly—many on the Left don't seem to raise their voices against the *current* slavery, discrimination, or forced labor camps existing in some of the totalitarian regimes of today. Coincidently, regimes that may make *some of them* collectively *billions of dollars in profit*, which enables their very lives of wealth, privilege, power, and…selective scorn against those they oppose.

As has been proven since recorded time: follow the money and you will often find the reason for the *silence*.

So, if you are a self-titled activist from the Left, why let the facts and the truth get in the way of your going back in time to *only attack* our 𝕱ounding 𝕱athers from the elite bubbles of your private jets, mansions, vacation homes in Tuscany, or tenured positions within the Ivy League?

"*The Ivy League.*"

A once proud and extolled hierarchy of education where now, the already ill-informed minds of students are often filled with "social justice warrior" edicts that will help them not in the least in making a living in the real world.

Of course, an equally worthwhile truth to note on this subject is that a number of these very pampered, elitist, out-of-touch-from-reality liberal students don't have to worry about finding a job. Or making money. *Ever.*

No. Thanks to very generous trust funds that will power their own entitlement and bias from the safety of their *inherited* elite bubbles, they can carry on tearing down—*sometimes literally, as anarchists in the streets*—those who either created and built our Republic, or those in the working class now trying to sustain it. As we say in the real world of fighting every day to pay the bills: "Nice work if you can get it."

Now, going back to the attacks on 𝕿homas 𝕵efferson from the Left.

Most revolve around the subject of slavery.

As mentioned, none of us will ever know what was really in the heart and soul of *Jefferson* at the time.

But, if we do go back *far enough* in time via research, there are at least some very credible hints as to where his mind was on that subject as well as a few others that directly impacted the lives and dignity of human beings.

Benson John Lossing. Mr. Lossing was born in 1813—while Jefferson was still alive—and became highly respected precisely because of his *insistence* on seeking out *only* the primary records of that time to bolster his own research and writing.

Lossing was such a stickler for using *only* primary information, firsthand accounts, and facts that the legendary Washington Irving once wrote to him to proclaim in part: "I have been gratified at finding how scrupulously attentive you have been to accuracy to facts, which is so essential in writings of an historical nature."

Indeed they are. Honesty and "accuracy to facts" are everything when recording *real* history. No one respected that duty to history more than Benson John Lossing.

With that reputation in mind, in 1848—fully thirteen years *before* the Civil War—Mr. Lossing wrote of **Thomas Jefferson**:

> From the early part of 1777 to the middle of 1779, Mr. Jefferson was assiduously employed...on a commission for revising the laws of Virginia. The duty was a most arduous one; and to Mr. Jefferson belongs the imperishable honor of being the first to propose, in the Legislature of Virginia, the laws forbidding the importation of slaves...establishing

schools for general education; and confirming
the rights of freedom in religious expression.[3]

Again, not only was this historical detail written thirteen
years *before* the Civil War but *only* twenty-two years *after* the
passing of Thomas Jefferson.

While many on the Left may outright refuse to accept it,
the fact is that Jefferson came to abhor the very idea of slavery
and his family's involvement in what we all know today to be
a "crime against humanity."

Regardless of whether the issue in 1776 was much more
complicated and nuanced that many would admit today, the
absolute fact was that it haunted Jefferson in one way or another for his remaining days on this Earth.

That internal disgust over the repulsive practice of slavery
was indeed upon his mind when he drafted these immortal
words that served as the very foundation for the Declaration of
Independence:

> We hold these truths to be self-evident, that
> all men are created equal.

How ironic, and yet how fitting, that come 1963, the courageous and heroic Civil Rights champion Dr. Martin Luther
King chose to recite those very same words in his historic and
iconic "I Have a Dream" speech.

CHAPTER ONE

"To the Men Who Did What Was Considered Wrong in Order to Do What They Knew Was Right!"

𝕿here is a very telling scene in the 2004 blockbuster movie titled *National Treasure*, a film that depicts a plot to steal the Declaration of Independence in order to *protect* it, where the Benjamin Franklin Gates character—played by Nicholas Cage—runs into Dr. Abigail Chase, an archivist for the National Archives—played by Diane Kruger—and her boorish male colleague.

The encounter takes place at a fundraising event at the National Archives—which houses the Declaration of Independence and other founding documents of the United States of America.

As Gates is at the National Archives at that *exact moment* to attempt to steal the Declaration of Independence, the last thing he wants or needs is to get distracted by either a woman he is already attracted to or her doting colleague, who is also clearly interested in her.

But because of the adrenaline running through him, his belief in doing the right things, and his sense of humorous irony, Gates cannot help himself and chooses that *exact* moment to make a toast to The 56 men who risked everything to sign the document he is about to steal.

Thanks to an equal amount of passion and champagne, Gates declares:

> A toast…to high treason. That's what these men were committing when they signed the Declaration. Had we lost the war, they would have been hanged, beheaded, drawn and quartered, and—Oh! Oh, my personal favorite—and had their entrails cut out and burned! So, here's to the men who did what was considered wrong in order to do what they knew was right. What they knew was right.

⁓

What they *knew* was right.

As noted, in the United States of *today*, more and more Americans are becoming more and more concerned about doing what "they know to be right" out of fear of either the cancel culture coming after them or even worse retribution being forced upon them for simply standing atop their *American* right to freely speak their minds.

Sadly, and now often tragically, they are correct to feel that way.

One of the beliefs most of these Americans share—men, women, and children who do believe in the rule of law, who do believe in the need for sovereign and protected borders, and who do believe in a loving God—is that those who risked their lives and the lives of their families to found the United States of America were patriots, heroes, and shining examples of the human species and the human spirit standing up—when almost no one else would out of fear of that barbaric retribution—against freedom-crushing tyranny.

Many of those who would gleefully cancel other Americans for simply speaking their minds or voicing a viewpoint contrary to their own also strongly reject the phrase "Founding Fathers."

They would either prefer to have the now politically correct "founders" used in its place or, as already stressed, have those men and their heroic actions censored or completely banned from the history of the United States of America. The very country *they* created.

And therein lies an even greater problem for those who believe that truth and history should *never, ever* be bent, twisted, censored, or banned to fit *any* particular narrative.

History—warts and all—is in fact *history*. Most especially, our *shared American history*.

It should never be altered or abolished. If it's good, let us praise it. If it is bad, let us condemn it and learn from it. But let us never bend, twist, censor, or ban it because it does not reflect a one-sided ideology of today.

As mentioned, as I write this book, the Left and even now the Far Left have a viselike grip on the major megaphones of our nation. Knowing that, and, as the cliché very accurately reminds us, "History is written—and *rewritten*, and *reimagined*—by the victors."

And make no mistake. As of now, the Left has *decisively won* the war for control over those institutions that do

influence—or dictate—so many of the governmental, political, and social decisions being made in our Republic today.
Dictates that we are also told time and again are "*for our
own good*."

Again, as *honest* history has recorded over the centuries,
when a government tells you it is forcefully subjugating your
basic human rights "*for your own good*," truly bad to outright
horrific things usually follow.

In light of that reality—and before this movement does
succeed in eradicating the lives, accomplishments, risks, and
very history of these heroic men—it seems fitting to not only
honor them, but to single out *one liberty*-promoting and -pro-
tecting lesson from *each* of the **56 Signers** who did courageously
risk their lives and all they had by putting their names to paper
when—as one—they signed the **Declaration of Independence**.

CHAPTER TWO

How American History Actually Happened

⛨ ruth *one* and history *one*: the **56** human beings who did
sign the **Declaration of Independence** were in fact...men.

Hence, the term "Founding Fathers."

Many today—including a number of conservatives and libertarians—most assuredly do wish there were signatures as well
from the "Manufacturing Mothers" on that historic document.

They may be correct to feel that way...*now.*

But that was not the reality...*then.*

I have no doubts in my mind that a number of the ideas,
suggestions, theories, and solutions that became the tenets of
our founding documents originated in the minds of the *women*
of that time.

Strong, courageous, and highly capable women who were
the wives, companions, or friends of the men who eventually
would draft and sign the **Declaration of Independence** and our
other founding documents.

Women, who would have either been privy to, or more
likely, were part of, lengthy conversations with the men involved
in the creation of those documents and...our very Republic.

No doubt, often brilliant women who helped to either shape the thoughts of the men behind those documents or steered them *away* from dangers and obstacles they themselves could not see or envision.

It simply defies human nature, logic, commonsense, and honesty not to believe that such conversations took place. Or that such conversations helped to positively guide the thoughts and the actions of the **56 Signers**.

While we can "never prove a negative," I am more than willing to stand behind that particular belief.

But no matter what I happen to believe *today*, the reality of *that time*—1776—was that the various power centers of the world were almost exclusively populated and controlled by…men.

That was the reality in 1776, in the decades and centuries *before* 1776, and for a century and more *after* 1776. Wishing it were not so or hating the fact that it was so does not *make* it not so.

But because the Left does now dominate the media, academia, and entertainment, some within those institutions have the natural temptation—simply, because they *can*—to alter, revise, or completely erase the actual truth and the actual history of a particular time solely because they happen to be in complete charge of that megaphone and are personally and ideologically offended by that past reality or those past truths.

While the instances of this type of bending, censoring, or banning of history continues to grow, thanks to the unchecked power they have, one particular example shows how effective—and damaging—such bending of history can be when orchestrated by a rightfully acclaimed and powerful filmmaker.

Back in November 2012, writer, director, and media mogul Steven Spielberg released his highly anticipated movie, *Lincoln*. The movie was *very* loosely based on the book from liberal "historian" Doris Kearns Goodwin titled *Team of Rivals: The Political Genius of Abraham Lincoln*.

That in turn quickly brings us back to what passes today for a "historian" for those who *do happen* to control the megaphones of our nation.

Not surprisingly, for the last couple of decades, those on the Left who control the media and academia *only* inserted their "hybrid" compilation of a "historian" into the various national debates and discussions. Male and female academics and authors who were alleged to be unbiased but who were in fact liberal to Far Left in their thinking.

However, once our nation entered the era of President Donald J. Trump in 2016, many of these same—already deeply biased individuals—became completely unhinged and cast aside *any* pretense of being objective.

One such person was Jon Meacham, the Pulitzer Prize–winning—a shamefully and *forever tarnished* award *only* given to liberals for decades—presidential "historian."

After then President Trump's Oval Office address on the need for a wall on our southern border, Meacham tweeted: "America should 'build a wall of steel, a wall as high as Heaven' against the flow of immigrants.—Gov. Clifford Walker, at a 1924 convention of the Ku Klux Klan, then a powerful force at a time of strain for the white working class."

Wow. A "historian" deliberately linking the then-president of the United States to the most vile, repugnant, and reviled organization in American history.

It should be noted that Meacham made no such comparison when President Barack Obama said: "We simply cannot allow people to pour into the United States undetected, undocumented, unchecked."[4] Or when Hillary Clinton admitted, "I voted, when I was a senator, to build a barrier to try to prevent illegal immigrants from coming in."[5]

As then-Senate Majority Leader Mitch McConnell stressed at that time: "The only things that have changed between then and now are the political winds, and of course, the occupant of the White House. So this is no newfound principled objection; it's just political spite. A partisan tantrum being prioritized over the public interest."[6]

Precisely. People have every right to despise or even hate former President Trump. That acknowledged, historians should never push opinions based on "political spite" or as part of a "partisan tantrum." As stated, history, the truth, and facts should never be bent or invented to favor one political party over the other or one ideology over another.

I happen to believe Meacham is an exceptional writer who has done some truly captivating and informative work. All the more reason to be disappointed to witness his then never-ending campaign to vilify Trump. As but another example, in his bestselling book, *The Soul of America: The Battle for Our Better Angels*, Meacham *opens with* a highly opinioned and clearly personal denouncement of Trump.

The Trump-hating *New York Times* praised the book by pointing out Meacham's mindset: "Appalled by the ascendancy of Donald J. Trump, and shaken by the deadly white nationalist rallies in Charlottesville in 2017, Meacham returns to other moments in history when fear and division seemed rampant." The Meacham-Trump narrative is now carved in granite.

Unfortunately, if you do take a few moments to research go-to "historians"—especially those the major networks and *CNN* and *MSNBC* often have on or quote—you would quickly see a clear bias among them in favor of liberal of Democratic politicians.

For instance, take this embarrassing exchange between "historian" Michael Beschloss and the late radio host Don Imus soon after Obama's 2008 election:

> Beschloss: "This is a guy [Obama] whose IQ is off the charts."
>
> Imus: "Well, what is his IQ?"
>
> Beschloss: "Pardon?"
>
> Imus: "What is his IQ?"
>
> Beschloss: "Uh, I would say it's probably— he's probably the smartest guy ever to become president."

On what—or *any*—actual evidence did the "unbiased historian" Beschloss base his assertion? The SAT scores Obama refused to release? The college transcripts he also kept private? Any existing IQ scores he withheld?

Barack Obama may in fact be incredibly "brilliant." But again, if you are going to make such a claim, what is *that* assertion based on?

Despite a lack of evidence, this highly acclaimed "historian" declared Obama smarter than George Washington,

Thomas Jefferson, Abraham Lincoln, John F. Kennedy, and Bill Clinton.

For sure, this was just a casual radio conversation. But it sounded more the opinion of an uninformed, starstruck teenybobber than a world-class, "impartial" historian.

It would be as if the *liberal* Noble Peace Prize had been awarded to a *just-elected* Obama in *the hope* he would make "extraordinary efforts to strengthen international diplomacy and cooperation between peoples." (Oh, wait—that actually *did happen*.)

Now, it's one thing if the far left Pulitzer and Nobel committees dive into the tank for liberal and socialist issues. That has long been accepted as the norm. But, it's quite another if professional "historians" join them.

After all, some of these liberal-leaning "historians," and most certainly Hollywood filmmakers, *do have* massive platforms and enormous power to *influence*. That's all the more reason they should never twist or reinvent history or facts to reflect their personal biases.

Which brings us back to writer and director Steven Spielberg and his film *Lincoln*.

By every single account, Steven Spielberg is an exceptionally good person who has truly helped tens of thousands of his fellow human beings with his kindness and generosity.

In my past life as director of communications for former Senator Bob Dole, I came up close and personal with Mr. Spielberg's kindness and generosity.

Back then, Bob Dole, among other things—"America's Veteran," former Senate majority leader, and presidential candidate—had been chairman of the World War Two Memorial Committee.

Both he and then FedEx chairman Fred Smith had been working tirelessly to raise private donations to build what many now consider to be the most striking, moving, and beautiful memorial in Washington, D.C.

One natural thought both men had was: *Gee. Since Hollywood studios collectively have made over a billion dollars in profit by making World War II movies over the decades, surely they would want to donate to a charity and a memorial honoring those who fought and died in a war that later enriched them all.*

As it turned out, not so much.

As in "No."

The conservation with various Hollywood elites usually went something like this:

> Bob Dole: "We are trying to build a memorial in Washington for our World War II vets using private funds and at no expense to the taxpayer. Sadly, at this time, *over one thousand World War II vets per day are dying*, so any immediate help would be greatly appreciated.

> Hollywood Executive: "Well, that sounds like a nice project, but it doesn't fit into our business plans at the moment, so we are going to decline to make a donation."

> Bob Dole: "Really? That's *ironic* because World War II didn't fit into *my* business plans at the time or the business plans of the over 400,000 Americans who lost their lives defending our nation while ensuring, among other things,

that you could still make movies and a huge profit. Thanks for taking my call."

Not surprisingly, we were told off-the-record that many in liberal Hollywood chose not to donate to the World War II Memorial precisely because its chairman—Bob Dole—was a *Republican*.

Now, let's contrast that bias, arrogance, ignorance, and selfishness with the incredible kindness, awareness, gratefulness, and sensitivity of Mr. Spielberg.

Besides trying to raise money to build the memorial, we needed to very quickly raise a substantial amount just to stage the groundbreaking ceremony.

Months earlier, knowing we had exactly zero dollars raised or committed for the purpose, I walked into Senator Dole's office and asked if he would mind if I reached out to Hollywood again.

He made a scowl at the suggestion, given the past rude reception he had gotten time and again from Hollywood elites but finally said, "If you want to waste your time with those ingrates, that's up to you."

Around that same time, I had struck up a working relationship with one of Mr. Spielberg's top people and decided I had nothing to lose by calling him. He, like me, had come out of the political world. Although, in his case, it was the liberal Democratic world.

His and my politics aside, from the very first day I spoke with him, he was always professional, classy, and a man of his word.

Once I got him on the phone this time, I explained our predicament in trying to raise money for the groundbreaking ceremony quickly coming up on November 11, 2000, Veterans Day.

I went into my, by-then practiced pitch, saying—begging—that if we could just get even one-eighth of the money needed for the groundbreaking ceremony, such a gift would be beyond helpful.

The high-level-staffer stopped me in midspiel. "Hold on a minute."

Less than a minute later, he was back on. But when he came back on the line, he had someone else with him on the call. That someone was Mr. Spielberg.

After getting over my nervousness about speaking with a legend, I started my pitch again: "Mr. Spielberg, if we could just get one-eighth of the amount needed to stage the groundbreaking ceremony…"

This time, it was Mr. Spielberg who stopped me.

"Doug, wait," he said. "What is the entire amount you need for the groundbreaking ceremony?"

We were so used to hearing "no" and then a dial tone from those in Hollywood, that I was honestly confused by the question.

"Pardon me, Mr. Spielberg," I began to say. "If you mean how much would one-eighth of the amount needed to fund the groundbreaking be…"

Mr. Spielberg stopped me with a warm laugh. "No, Doug. I'm asking you how much the *entire* groundbreaking ceremony would cost. What's the full amount needed to fund all of it?"

I took a deep breath, let it out very slowly, and answered: "The full amount we need to fund the entire groundbreaking ceremony is…six hundred and fifteen thousand dollars."

"No problem," answered Mr. Spielberg. "We will FedEx you the full amount tomorrow. The World War II Memorial is incredibly important to our nation and our history, and we are proud to be a small part of it with this donation. Please let me know if we can help with anything else."

I was honestly dumbstruck and simply stared down at the phone for a minute after the call ended.

True to his word, the next day, a check for $615,000—in care of my attention—landed on my desk.

With one incredibly generous donation, Mr. Spielberg helped to erase some of the pettiness and unneeded partisanship of a number of his Hollywood colleagues.

Simply, an off-the-charts act of kindness from one who has helped so many over the years.

All of that took place early in the year 2000.

Again, there is no doubt that Mr. Spielberg remains the same very kind, very generous, and very aware man today. Maybe even more so.

That said, seemingly every year since 2000, the politics in our nation have become more polarized, more accusatory, and much more tribal and personal.

Twelve years later in 2012—after the confusion and anger regarding the George W. Bush-Al Gore election combined with the first four years of President Barack Obama—things had gotten decidedly more partisan and acrimonious.

Symbolically, Mr. Spielberg released his movie *Lincoln* over the Veterans Day weekend in 2012. Basically twelve years to the day after the groundbreaking ceremony for the World War II Memorial that he personally and graciously funded.

By 2012 had Mr. Spielberg become more political or partisan since I had spoken with him in 2000? I honestly have no idea.

That said, my suspicion is that Mr. Spielberg is not a partisan at all and is really just a truly brilliant filmmaker at heart who can maybe get caught up in the political or partisan heat of the moment.

Partisan or not, Mr. Spielberg has let it be known over the years that he is a Democrat and does support Democratic or liberal-leaning candidates and positions. And again, there is absolutely *nothing wrong with that.*

In fact, there's everything *correct* with that in the sense that he is exercising his rights as an American citizen.

As of this writing, this still is the United States of America and Mr. Spielberg has the right to be liberal, conservative, or politically agnostic.

Ironically, most Republicans and conservatives do happen to support that belief. A sentiment regarding our constitutionally guaranteed and protected rights many others vehemently disagree with when it comes to conservatives voicing *their* opinions.

Especially, it seems...in *Hollywood.* I find it impossible to believe that Mr. Spielberg remotely supports the discrimination openly employed within his own industry against conservatives, Republicans, or people of traditional faith.

That said, Mr. Spielberg—as a proud liberal—does have the right to voice his opinion on *any* subject of his choosing.

What he, or anyone else, *does not have the right to do*—most especially because of his internationally powerful platform—is *revise* or *bend* history because that might be how he or some other liberals *wish* it had been as opposed to how it *actually was* during that time period in the United States.

Unfortunately, with the very opening scene of *Lincoln*, Mr. Spielberg and his liberal screenwriter chose to revise or *reimagine* history to fit neatly into some of the narratives of 2012 as opposed to the truths—ugly as they may have been—of 1864.

In a "We have been artificially forced together to make a political statement" moment, two lowly and poor Union soldiers—one black and one white—are standing together when they are *magically approached* by President Abraham Lincoln. This meeting never happened—the liberal screenwriter created it out of whole cloth.

But not satisfied with inventing that bit of history, the writer doubled-down by having the two *fictional* Union soldiers lovingly and worshipfully recite the words of Lincoln's Gettysburg address to...*Lincoln*.

Seriously. Are you *kidding* me?

This is a glaring example of why *every* writer—even the most talented on Earth—needs not only an editor but also...a reality check from time to time.

One assumes that Mr. Spielberg and his liberal writer knew that the Gettysburg Address by Lincoln did not become famous or well-known until decades *after* the Civil War. But again, if you have the money and power to revise or invent American history with no one to stop you, why not go ahead and have at it?

Ironically, at Gettysburg itself in 2012, when addressing the historical *liberties* taken with the film *Lincoln*, Mr. Spielberg himself admitted that it is the job of a filmmaker to use creative "imagination." A process that Mr. Spielberg also said could be interpreted as: "This resurrection is a fantasy...a dream."

A more accurate way to interpret those words might be: It's a "liberal fantasy" and a "liberal dream."

But what happens when Americans—who are no longer taught *real American history* in school—can no longer tell the difference between a "fantasy," a "dream," and...the actual truthful history of their nation that *did* take place? As flawed or repulsive as it may have been.

To be sure, at some point all filmmakers and authors must use some degree of "creative license" to tell parts of a story. But when you are telling the story of very real and sometimes very painful history of the United States, you have *zero right* to invent what you know to be untrue or inaccurate for that time.

It's deceitful and wrong and plants the seeds of confusion.

To this very point, a review of the film in the *Jewish Daily Forward* from November 2012 titled "Spielberg's Portrait of Lincoln Is a Bust," spoke to this very issue. Observed the reviewer in part:[7]

> My suspicion that Steven Spielberg can't really do historical films isn't anything new.... Maybe this is because narrative, clarity, and fluidity always count for more with Spielberg than historical precision.... I think that part of what keeps *Lincoln* so far away from any mythical past I can believe in is a form of Political Correctness that often resembles petrification. It's so hot and bothered about getting things wrong that it can't find many ways of getting things right. For starters, most of the black characters in this story—including the private and corporal Union soldiers—both apparently

fictional—who are shown in the first scene meeting Lincoln and then proudly quoting him—are plainly 20th Century figures in speech and body language, not inhabitants of the 19th Century....

Again. Precisely.

It was not how American history *actually* happened. In this particular case and in this particular movie, it was how those associated with that film wished or "dreamed" it would happen.

As was the closing scene of the movie where First Lady Mary Lincoln and her Black servant seat themselves in the House Gallery to observe firsthand the final tally on the vote for the Thirteenth Amendment.

As with the opening scene with the two *fictional* Union soldiers reciting the Gettysburg Address to Lincoln, those behind the film knew neither Mary Lincoln nor her servant ever sat in the House Gallery. And yet, they could not help themselves. They wanted to revise and bend American history to match certain narratives of 2012.

Those opening and closing scenes of *Lincoln* serve as perfect bookends of a revision or reimagining of actual US history. A revision that *did* succeed in confusing contemporary Americans regarding the past real history of their nation.

As those worried about the bending or deliberate blurring of US history soon discovered, many people who watched the movie *Lincoln*—then and now—truly believe that those events, as well as a number of other fictional inventions in the film, did in fact occur.

This reality shows that one person's idealistic, "do-good" revisionist can be another's irresponsible ideological propagandist.

American history should *never* be bent, revised, or banned to fit *any* particular narrative. Ever.

Once again, history—warts and all—is in fact, *history*. Our *American history* should never be altered or abolished.

Just to complete the circle on Mr. Spielberg and censorship, we have this truly interesting bit of ironic timing.

Almost everyone knows of his 1982 movie, *E.T.: The Extra-Terrestrial*. Most consider it a cinematic and Spielberg masterpiece of filmmaking that blended the minds of children and adults into a wonderful sci-fi "What if?"

Come 2002, people—most especially children who grew up with the film and now wanted to introduce their own children to this part of *their* life—were incredibly anxious to see the twentieth anniversary rerelease of the movie.

But, by the thousands, as they now watched this rerelease with their own children, those adults began to realize that something about the film had *dramatically changed* since they first viewed and loved it two decades before.

That something was that Steven Spielberg decided to *censor* his very own movie. Seemingly bending to the will of "anti-gun" voices, Mr. Spielberg decided to digitally remove the *handguns* being carried by FBI agents in the film and then digitally replace them with…*walkie-talkies*.

Some critics later joked that Spielberg was "Lucas-ing" his own movie. That was a reference to George Lucas censoring his own *Star Wars* movie to appease his own liberal league of overly sensitive viewers.

Ironically, come 2012, Mr. Spielberg realized the error of his ways by *uncensoring* the movie he had *censored* ten years earlier.

Speaking at a screening for the thirtieth anniversary of *Indiana Jones*, Mr. Spielberg decided to address the censorship he had inflicted upon his own *E.T.* masterpiece a decade before. Said Mr. Spielberg to the audience before him via news reports from the time:

> For myself, I tried [changing a film] once and lived to regret it. Not because of fan outrage, but because I was disappointed in myself. I got overly sensitive to [some of the reaction] to E.T., and I thought if technology evolved [I might go in and change some things]...it was OK for a while, but I realized what I had done was I had robbed people who loved E.T. of their memories of E.T. [...] If I put just one cut of E.T. on Blu-ray and it was the 1982, would anyone object to that? [The crowd yells "NO!" in unison.] OK, so be it.[8]

So, come 2012 and the thirtieth anniversary rerelease of *E.T.*, Mr. Spielberg removed the offending, digitally added, politically correct–induced walkie-talkies and *restored* the handguns the FBI agents in the movie had been carrying before self- and forced censorship got the better of him and his judgment.

But in one of those "you couldn't make it up if you tried" timing moments, Mr. Spielberg spoke of his "regret" and being "disappointed" in himself over *that act of censorship and revisionism* approximately *one month before* the release of his movie *Lincoln*.

The unspoken message seemed to be: "Some censorship and revision of history may be warranted if it advances a political or ideological narrative."

Maybe now in 2022, with the tenth anniversary of *Lincoln*, Mr. Spielberg will admit to some "regret" and "disappointment" in himself for altering *real* American history to fictionally create a "I wish it were that way then" narrative that continues to mislead many who see what is still an incredibly well-made and well-acted film.

I have no doubt that somewhere within himself, Mr. Spielberg knows that the censoring and revising of American history for *any* reason—most of all, political—is wrong and a line that must never be crossed.

When that belief does once again fill his mind, we can only hope he will pass along that message to the countless liberal to far-left filmmakers now working overtime to revise or erase other instances of *real American history* along with... *real Americans*.

༄

Now, with all of that stated, and with as much accuracy, respect, and gratitude as possible, what follows are reverential snapshots of the **56 Signers** who not only forever affixed their names to the **Declaration of Independence** but also, in the process, did create the greatest, most free, and most fair nation the world has ever known.

Long may the vision of those **56 Signers** survive.

CHAPTER THREE

The Declaration of Independence…
in its Own Words

But before we do get to those men, let's revisit *their vision* as well as their *collective genius* via the very document they did sign to give birth to our nation.

Many times, when a book is referencing the 𝔇𝔢𝔠𝔩𝔞𝔯𝔞𝔱𝔦𝔬𝔫 𝔬𝔣 𝔍𝔫𝔡𝔢𝔭𝔢𝔫𝔡𝔢𝔫𝔠𝔢 or any of our founding documents, some authors or publishers tend to bury those documents in the back of the book or make them an appendage in the back of the book.

Well…not *this* book.

This document, these heroic men, and this noble history should never be an afterthought or lumped in with reference material next to some boring or ignored index. It is reproduced below exactly with the spelling and syntax of that time.

THE DECLARATION OF INDEPENDENCE

IN CONGRESS, JULY 4, 1776

The unanimous Declaration of the thirteen United States of America

When in the Course of human events, it becomes necessary for one people to dissolve the political bands which have connected them with another, and to assume among the powers of the earth, the separate and equal station to which the Laws of Nature and of Nature's God entitle them, a decent respect to the opinions of mankind requires that they should declare the causes which impel them to the separation.

We hold these truths to be self-evident, that all men are created equal, that they are endowed by their Creator with certain unalienable Rights, that among these are Life, Liberty and the pursuit of Happiness.--That to secure these rights, Governments are instituted among Men, deriving their just powers from the consent of the governed,--That whenever any Form of Government becomes destructive of these ends, it is the Right of the People to alter or to abolish it, and to institute new Government, laying its foundation on such principles and organizing its powers in such form, as to them shall seem most likely to effect their Safety and Happiness. Prudence, indeed, will dictate that Governments long established should not be changed for light and transient causes; and accordingly all experience hath shewn, that mankind are more disposed to suffer, while evils are sufferable, than

41

to right themselves by abolishing the forms to which they are accustomed. But when a long train of abuses and usurpations, pursuing invariably the same Object evinces a design to reduce them under absolute Despotism, it is their right, it is their duty, to throw off such Government, and to provide new Guards for their future security.--Such has been the patient sufferance of these Colonies; and such is now the necessity which constrains them to alter their former Systems of Government. The history of the present King of Great Britain is a history of repeated injuries and usurpations, all having in direct object the establishment of an absolute Tyranny over these States. To prove this, let Facts be submitted to a candid world.

He has refused his Assent to Laws, the most wholesome and necessary for the public good.

He has forbidden his Governors to pass Laws of immediate and pressing importance, unless suspended in their operation till his Assent should be obtained; and when so suspended, he has utterly neglected to attend to them.

He has refused to pass other Laws for the accommodation of large districts of people, unless those people would relinquish the right of Representation in the Legislature, a right inestimable to them and formidable to tyrants only.

He has called together legislative bodies at places unusual, uncomfortable, and distant from the depository of their public Records, for the sole purpose of fatiguing them into compliance with his measures.

He has dissolved Representative Houses repeatedly, for opposing with manly firmness his invasions on the rights of the people.

He has refused for a long time, after such dissolutions, to cause others to be elected; whereby the Legislative powers, incapable of Annihilation, have returned to the People at large for their exercise; the State remaining in the mean time exposed to all the dangers of invasion from without, and convulsions within.

He has endeavoured to prevent the population of these States; for that purpose obstructing the Laws for Naturalization of Foreigners; refusing to pass others to encourage their migrations hither, and raising the conditions of new Appropriations of Lands.

He has obstructed the Administration of Justice, by refusing his Assent to Laws for establishing Judiciary powers.

He has made Judges dependent on his Will alone, for the tenure of their offices, and the amount and payment of their salaries.

He has erected a multitude of New Offices, and sent hither swarms of Officers to harrass our people, and eat out their substance.

He has kept among us, in times of peace, Standing Armies without the Consent of our legislatures.

He has affected to render the Military independent of and superior to the Civil power.

He has combined with others to subject us to a jurisdiction foreign to our constitution, and unacknowledged by our laws; giving his Assent to their Acts of pretended Legislation:

For Quartering large bodies of armed troops among us:

For protecting them, by a mock Trial, from punishment for any Murders which they should commit on the Inhabitants of these States:

For cutting off our Trade with all parts of the world:

For imposing Taxes on us without our Consent:

For depriving us in many cases, of the benefits of Trial by Jury:

For transporting us beyond Seas to be tried for pretended offences

For abolishing the free System of English Laws in a neighbouring Province, establishing therein an Arbitrary government, and enlarging its Boundaries so as to render it at once an example and fit instrument for introducing the same absolute rule into these Colonies:

For taking away our Charters, abolishing our most valuable Laws, and altering fundamentally the Forms of our Governments:

For suspending our own Legislatures, and declaring themselves invested with power to legislate for us in all cases whatsoever.

He has abdicated Government here, by declaring us out of his Protection and waging War against us.

He has plundered our seas, ravaged our Coasts, burnt our towns, and destroyed the lives of our people.

He is at this time transporting large Armies of foreign Mercenaries to compleat the works of death, desolation and tyranny, already begun with circumstances of Cruelty & perfidy scarcely paralleled in the most barbarous ages, and totally unworthy the Head of a civilized nation.

He has constrained our fellow Citizens taken Captive on the high Seas to bear Arms against their Country, to become the executioners of their friends and Brethren, or to fall themselves by their Hands.

He has excited domestic insurrections amongst us, and has endeavoured to bring on the inhabitants of our frontiers, the merciless Indian Savages, whose known rule of warfare, is an undistinguished destruction of all ages, sexes and conditions.

In every stage of these Oppressions We have Petitioned for Redress in the most humble terms: Our repeated Petitions have been answered only by repeated injury. A Prince whose character is thus marked by every act which may define a Tyrant, is unfit to be the ruler of a free people.

Nor have We been wanting in attentions to our Brittish brethren. We have warned them from time to time of attempts by their legislature to extend an unwarrantable jurisdiction over us. We have reminded them of the circumstances of our emigration and settlement here. We have appealed to their native justice and magnanimity, and we have conjured them by the ties of our common kindred to disavow these usurpations, which, would inevitably interrupt our connections and correspondence. They too have been deaf to the voice of justice and of consanguinity. We must, therefore, acquiesce in the necessity, which denounces our Separation, and hold them, as we hold the rest of mankind, Enemies in War, in Peace Friends.

We, therefore, the Representatives of the united States of America, in General Congress, Assembled, appealing to the Supreme Judge of the world for the rectitude of our intentions, do, in the Name, and by Authority of the good People of these Colonies, solemnly publish and declare, That these United Colonies are, and of Right ought to be Free and Independent States; that they are Absolved from all Allegiance to the British Crown, and that all political connection between them and the State of Great Britain, is and ought to be totally dissolved; and that as Free and Independent States, they have full Power to levy War, conclude Peace, contract Alliances, establish Commerce, and to do all other Acts and Things which Independent States may of right do. And for the *support of this Declaration, with a firm reliance on the protection of divine Providence, we mutually pledge to each other our Lives, our Fortunes and our sacred Honor.*

2‰

Now, going back to the movie *National Treasure*, there is a critically important exchange between the Benjamin Franklin Gates character and the Riley character as they are standing in the National Archives looking down upon the **Declaration of Independence**:

> Benjamin Franklin Gates: "Of all the words written here about freedom, there's a line here that's at the heart of all the others:
>
> 'But when a long train of abuses and usurpations, pursuing invariably the same object, evinces a design to reduce them under absolute despotism, it is their right, it is their duty to throw off such government and provide new guards for their future security.'
>
> "People don't talk that way anymore."
>
> Riley: "No idea what you said."
>
> Benjamin Franklin Gates: "It means, if there's something wrong, those who have the ability to take action *have the responsibility to take action*."

ↄ乃

Obviously, those fighting tyranny, oppression, and discrimination back in 1776 were clearly made of much sterner stuff than many of the elites of today who profess their belief in the **Declaration of Independence** and their love of liberty and yet... choose nonaction while enjoying their great wealth.

In 1776, the Patriots of that era had to put their *actual lives* on the line to literally fight for their rights and their freedom. Today, in order to save the nation created by these **56 Signers** and others, "those who have the ability to take action," *need only create* fair, honest, and unbiased centers for media, academia, entertainment, science, and medicine.

Not too much to ask in comparison to the life-taking risks faced by the **Founding Fathers** of our Republic. And yet, rather than enthusiastically come forward to protect *their* freedoms and rights and those of their families by creating honest and fair megaphones—most with the means and the power to "take action"—still deliberately choose to "*be with those cold and timid souls who neither know victory nor defeat.*"

Except as the **56 Signers** from 1776 would have been honor bound to warn them, that strategy of self-serving *inaction* will still *only* lead to "defeat" and then...complete surrender to a dictatorial dominion out of their worst nightmares.

Again, and to paraphrase Pastor Niemöller:

> Then, as an ultrawealthy, powerful, and influential conservative, libertarian, or person of traditional faith living within the protected

bubble of privilege the autocrats allowed me, they came for me—and there was no one left to speak for me.

But...I digress.

Part Two

PROFILES OF THE 56 SIGNERS

AUTHOR'S NOTE

𝕭efore diving into the actual lives and accomplishments of the signers, I think a little explanation is in order.

The first order of business is the discrepancy between the number of signers and the number of biographies presented here. Everyone knows that there were **56 Signers** of the **Declaration of Independence**. That's true, but for the purposes of this book I have decided to add a "plus one," **Robert R. Livingston.** Livingstone was an integral part of the committee to *draft* the Declaration, but he was quite unfairly unable to *sign it* based on circumstances completely out of his control. Knowing that, perhaps a more accurate title for this book would be **The 56**...*Accompanied by a "Plus One."*

Next, a word about the order in which I have presented the signers might be instructive. While each and every man who put pen to paper to sign the **Declaration of Independence** was truly courageous for a number of reasons, I believe that *seven men* (**Richard Henry Lee, Thomas Jefferson, John Hancock, Benjamin Franklin, John Adams, Robert R. Livingston,** and **Roger Sherman**) should be recognized before all others, given their actual roles in bringing that founding document and our country to life.

And from *that* number, *three* (Lee, Jefferson, and Hancock) come before the following four. And from those four, *one* (Franklin) appears before the other three (Adams, Livingston, and Sherman).

The last two names of the seven men most responsible for bringing the **Declaration of Independence** to life (**Livingston** and **Sherman**) deserve a special note. These two highly gifted **Founding Fathers** are sometimes literally ignored or forgotten by some retelling the history of that time. There are several examples of this. All basically show the same disrespect by stating something along the lines of: "**John Adams, Benjamin Franklin, Thomas Jefferson,** *and two others* were picked to oversee the draft of the **Declaration of Independence.**"

"*...and two others.*" Are you kidding me? How difficult or time consuming would it have been to list the names of the two **Founding Fathers** who were named to the Committee of Five to draft the **Declaration of Independence?** The immensely impressive **Robert R. Livingston,** as stated above my plus one, is a name that must always be remembered and spoken about when discussing not only the drafting of our **Declaration of Independence** but also the very birth of our nation.

The second of the "two others," **Roger Sherman,** also deserves to have his name specifically remembered as a Patriot who helped bring about the Declaration of Independence, as you will read more about in Chapter Ten.

Following these seven impressive founders come the **Final Fifty** signers, with a special nod to the remarkable contributions of the other Adams, **Samuel Adams,** to start with.

Now, let's find out more about these remarkable Patriots.

CHAPTER FOUR

Richard Henry Lee

In my honestly very humble opinion, the first who should be recognized above all others is a man whom even most Americans who do cherish the **Declaration of Independence** may either not know or only have a passing knowledge him. That Patriot from Virginia is **Richard Henry Lee**.

"*Who*?" some might already be asking.

Before getting into some of the brief particulars on the truly amazing life of **Richard Henry Lee**, we need to cut to the chase as to why I believe he should be the *first* among **The 56**.

While much of history, or even *all* in certain circumstances, can be open to debate and interpretation, there is little doubt that **Richard Henry Lee** was ultimately one of the main architects behind both, the push for independence from "Great Britain," as well as the very need to draft and put forth a formal **Declaration of Independence**.

For over two centuries now, Americans have come to associate the names of **Thomas Jefferson**, **Benjamin Franklin**, **John Adams**, and **John Hancock** with our most sacred of Founding documents.

To be sure, all those men played critical roles and more. But within the giant shadows those signers cast was a man who did much of the prep work needed to reach those "Revolutionary" milestones.

That man was 𝕽𝖎𝖈𝖍𝖆𝖗𝖉 𝕳𝖊𝖓𝖗𝖞 𝕷𝖊𝖊. He should be first among equals because, when an act of pure clarity and courage was needed, it was he who first jumped into the arena when others about him were understandably nervous or outright petrified by the idea of articulating "independence" from "Great Britain."

𝕽𝖎𝖈𝖍𝖆𝖗𝖉 𝕳𝖊𝖓𝖗𝖞 𝕷𝖊𝖊 was first sent from Virginia to the Continental Congress in 1774. From the moment he arrived, there were murmurings to pointed conversations to debates to full-blown arguments about the need for the colonies to dissolve all political and governmental connections with the "mother country."

But even such private conversations, debates, and arguments were dangerous to those engaged in them. One of the main reasons being the prying eyes and ears of the "Loyalists" to the Crown.

Loyalists were generally well-off to wealthy citizens of the then-thirteen colonies who could and *did* morph into collaborators to curry favor or reward from the Crown.

Informing on secretive discussions regarding the possibility of independence from Great Britain was one of the foremost guaranteed ways to receive such favor or reward.

Every member of the Continental Congress was not only aware of that reality but also knew full well the gruesome punishment the British would inflict for such a "treasonous act."

Hence, the understandable hesitancy of one to *volunteer* to not only publicly articulate that which all believed must be said but also, in reality, *voluntarily* place one's head on the chopping block for a Crown executioner to lop off at a future date.

At the Continental Congress meeting of 𝕵𝖚𝖓𝖊 7, 1776, the delegation from Virginia was unanimous in agreement that a "declaration of independence from Great Britain" should be proposed. It was quite another thing for someone to stand up, step up, and offer it.

𝕽𝖎𝖈𝖍𝖆𝖗𝖉 𝕳𝖊𝖓𝖗𝖞 𝕷𝖊𝖊 truly felt the hand of destiny was resting upon his shoulder. It was a hand that may have been placed there two years earlier when the Crown punished the city of Boston for their "insolent" act of rebellion in the form of the Boston Tea Party. It was a hand that independently but almost simultaneously with another Founding Father pushed the need for "committees of correspondence" that would allow the colonies to communicate with each other.

With each passing day, Lee was coming to believe that the dictatorial iron grip of the Crown was never going to stop closing around the throat of the colonies until all oxygen had been cut off.

Before almost all, Lee came to believe that the *only* legitimate chance to survive the ever-tightening grip of the Crown oppressors was to declare independence from Great Britain and form a new and free Republic.

With that belief now permanently settled within his mind for the last two-plus years, Lee came forth at that Continental Congress on 𝕵𝖚𝖓𝖊 7, 1776, to offer the resolution. Words and a resolution that would make and change history.

Said Lee: "*That these united colonies are, and of right, ought to be, free and independent states; and that all political connections between them and the state of Great Britain is, and ought to be, totally dissolved.*"[9]

Done.

The fuse of liberty had been lit.

But again, at great risk to whomever stepped up with the rhetorical torch to light said fuse. As was recorded soon afterward.

The membership of the Continental Congress was well aware of the mortal danger 𝕽𝖎𝖈𝖍𝖆𝖗𝖉 𝕳𝖊𝖓𝖗𝖞 𝕷𝖊𝖊 had just brought upon himself. So much so that they decided to initially strike his name from the official record.

As was reported:

> Congress being of opinion that the member who made the first mention on the subject of independence would certainly be exposed to personal and imminent danger, directed its Secretary to omit the name of the mover... The name of, neither of him who moved the resolution, nor of him who seconded them, was mentioned.[10]

The man who "seconded" Lee's resolution was 𝕵𝖔𝖍𝖓 𝕬𝖉𝖆𝖒𝖘.

But, in spite of knowing the danger to his life, Lee was far from finished. He still felt it was his sacred duty to convince the more reluctant members of the Continental Congress to adopt the only viable course before them if they wanted to secure true liberty for themselves and their families.

In remarks backing his resolution, Lee offered up some of the most courageous and inspiring words in the history of our Republic. Said Mr. Lee in part:

Why then, Sir, do we longer delay? Why still deliberate? Let her arise, not to devastate and conquer, but to re-establish the reign of peace and law. The eyes of Europe are fixed upon us; she demands of us a living example of freedom, that may exhibit a contrast, in the felicity of the citizen, to the ever-increasing tyranny which desolates her polluted shores. She invites us to prepare an asylum, where the unhappy may find solace, and the persecuted repose. She entreats us to cultivate a propitious soil, where that genuine plant; which first sprang and grew in England, but is now withered by the blasts of tyranny, may revive and flourish, sheltering under its salubrious and interminable shade all the unfortunate of the human race. If we are not this day wanting in our duty to our country, the names of the American legislators of '76 will be placed by posterity at the side of those of Theseus, of Lycurgus, of Romulus, of Numa, of the three Williams of Nassau, and of all those whose memory has been, and forever will be, dear to virtuous men and good citizens.[11]

In other words, the names of others throughout history were willing to jump into that arena Teddy Roosevelt would immortalize in another speech 134 years later.

And now *today*, 112 years after the iconic Roosevelt speech, and after watching liberty, individual rights, and other freedoms surreally but *instantly being* taken from us and others in "first world" countries around the world during these last few years by certain politicians and unelected bureaucrats—"for our own good"—Lee's remarks supporting his resolution ring just as loud now for tens of millions of Americans and hundreds of millions of people around the world. Hard-working, law-abiding human beings who witnessed the often twisted, power-hungry faces of those pushing tyrannical dictates rise up before them from the depths of their worst nightmares.

Beginning early in 2020, it was the reaction to the pandemic—*not*, the pandemic itself—that gave birth to instant overreach that robbed so many of their rights, freedoms, and livelihoods.

But, you may ask, how could so many first-world countries around the world fall victim to such one-sided, power-hungry groupthink?

Quite easily and very logically, actually.

Like the United States, many countries around the world—such as Canada, the United Kingdom, Germany, France, Australia, New Zealand, and Spain—have their particular megaphones of the media, academia, entertainment, science, and medicine also *overwhelmingly dominated* by the Left and the Far Left. All those highly biased and often corrupt megaphones then easily influence tens of other nations around the world to succumb to orchestrated panic and draconian dictates.

Suddenly—and for as long as they deem it's needed—*their* particular form of "groupthink becomes the *literal* law of the land.

Refuse to wear a mask *outside* and a reptilian brown-shirt police officer will literally choke you. *Peacefully* question the need for a vaccine mandate and another reptilian brown-shirt police officer will cowardly sneak up to you from behind, lock your arms, and slam you face-first into the granite floor as your skull cracks from the impact and blood and urine pour from your now-unconscious body.

As hundreds of such atrocities occurred, most of the liberal mainstream media and liberal politicians chose to ignore them.

They got away with it because there are *no* established, pragmatic, and honest megaphones to challenge those dictates and invented laws.

As the cliché asks: "If a tree falls in the forest and nobody is there to hear it, does it make a sound?"

As these last few years have made clear, the answer to that wise and needed question is a resoundingly loud "no."

Because when you *do* control the megaphones that *control* the people…you can also purposely sow more confusion and harm simply by *omission*. *Don't* report the truth. *Don't* report dissenting opinion. *Don't* give voice to highly reputable scientists or experts. *Don't*.

Food for thought: These last few years, the crisis that allowed the elites to deprive the masses of so many of their rights, freedoms, and livelihoods was the pandemic.

Seeing how incredibly easy it was to manipulate the masses to "voluntarily" give up so many of their God-given rights via the megaphones they control—while making billions of dollars in the process—what's the next and bigger "crisis" some on the Left may attempt to roll out to further solidify their power and financial interests?

"*Climate change*," anyone? Some believe the pandemic provided the perfect "*for your own good*" dress rehearsal for the ultimate dictatorial power grab.

Now, with that dictatorial overreach firmly in mind, back to the Patriot who put all on the line to revive the plant of liberty "*now withered by the blasts of tyranny.*"

❧

As noted by the National Archives and others, that not for illness within his family, **Richard Henry Lee** would not only have been a member of the committee delegated by the Continental Congress to draft the Declaration of Independence, but also he would have been named its *chairman*.

He was the driving force behind that momentum.

Sadly, on **June 10, 1776**, word reached Lee that his wife—the former Anne Gaskins Pinckard—was gravely ill.

Lee left Philadelphia immediately to be by her side.

The very next day, while greatly missing Lee but under *his* instructions to continue in his absence, the Continental Congress did indeed pick the committee to draft a declaration of independence.

That committee consisted of **Thomas Jefferson** of Virginia, **Benjamin Franklin** of Pennsylvania, **John Adams** of Massachusetts, **Robert R. Livingston** of New York, and **Roger Sherman** of Connecticut.

All names today—in 2022—that are being subjected to various forms of attack, censorship, or outright banishment by many from the Left.

With Lee on the way back to Virginia, the Continental Congress quickly named **Thomas Jefferson** not only as the

chairman of the committee to draft a declaration of independence, but also assigned him the duty of *writing the draft* for
the others in the committee to edit before presenting it to the
whole of the Continental Congress.

Again, two honors that would have most assuredly fallen
upon Lee had he been able to remain in Philadelphia.

To underscore that point while reinforcing Lee's critical
role in not only the push for liberty but also the need for a
declaration of independence, we have the words of 𝔍𝔬𝔥𝔫 𝔄𝔡𝔞𝔪𝔰.

Again, Mr. Adams not only bravely seconded the resolution put forth by Lee, but after action on it had been de-
ferred by the Continental Congress for three weeks, quite
successfully defended it to that body and on 𝔍𝔲𝔩𝔶 2, 1776, the
United Colonies of America officially became the United
States of America.

Because of Lee's resolution being adopted on *that day*,
𝔍𝔬𝔥𝔫 𝔄𝔡𝔞𝔪𝔰 truly believed that July 2 would be the day all
future generations of Americans would celebrate as the birth
of their nation.

Said Adams in a letter to his wife Abigail dated 𝔍𝔲𝔩𝔶 3, 1776:

> The Second Day of July, 1776 will be the
> most memorable Epocha in the History of
> America…It ought to be solemnized with
> Pomp and Parade, with Shews, Games, Sports,
> Guns, Bells, Bonfires, and Illuminations from
> one end of the Continent to the other from
> this Time forward forever more.[12]

It was not. 𝔍𝔲𝔩𝔶 4 became that day. But as it has been noted
in the past, if the signing of the 𝔇𝔢𝔠𝔩𝔞𝔯𝔞𝔱𝔦𝔬𝔫 𝔬𝔣 𝔍𝔫𝔡𝔢𝔭𝔢𝔫𝔡𝔢𝔫𝔠𝔢 was

our Republic's birth announcement, then surely **Richard Henry Lee's** resolution was its *birth certificate*.

꒰

As for Lee himself, what follows is a bit of his personal history.

He was born in the county of Westmoreland, Virginia, on **January 20, 1732.**

Like a number of the **56 Signers**, he—and his brother who was *also* a signer—was born into a comfortable life that represented the upper ranks of the colonies. As such, Lee's father did what many financially comfortable to very well-off families did at the time: send Lee back to England at a very young age to be formally educated.

In a bit of irony when it comes to the trustworthiness of the "historians" featured by the Left in today's mainstream media and academia, Lee was deeply interested in the history of the world prior to his arrival in it and became a voracious consumer of any and all texts he could get his hands on that spoke to the history of the most powerful empires and countries the world had known up until that time.

Yet another reason why Lee became convinced that the colonies had to seek complete and total independence from Great Britain. He truly did understand the honest history of the world, and he truly did believe that those who did not learn from it were condemned to repeat it.

As to yet *another reason* why Lee might be the first among equals when it comes to the **56 Signers** is the fact that he was also the driving force behind the creation of our **Bill of Rights**.

Richard Henry Lee had long been known as an anti-Federalist. That is, he believed the power of the people should remain primarily with state and local governments and not in the hands of an all-powerful federal government.

For that very reason, Lee and others like him, believed that the United States Constitution needed to have a Bill of Rights to safeguard the individual liberties of the citizens of the Republic.

Lee so strongly insisted upon this protection of individual liberties that when he was elected to the Constitutional Convention of 1787, he flat-out refused to attend because there was no agreement to add such a Bill of Rights.

Four years later in 1791, that Bill of Rights—which Lee tirelessly campaigned to make a reality—was finally added to the Constitution of the United States. The Bill of Rights at the time was made up of the first Ten Amendments to that Constitution. The First Amendment guaranteed the ability to speak and worship freely, and the Fourth Amendment—*which should echo quite loudly in our current times*—safeguarded the rights of citizens *to be free from unreasonable government intrusion* in their homes through the requirement of a warrant.

Richard Henry Lee passed in 1794 at the age of sixty-two.

Our Republic's debt to him, his courage, and his lasting vision for our very liberties and freedom is immeasurable.

CHAPTER FIVE

Thomas Jefferson

How brilliant was the mind of 𝕿𝖍𝖔𝖒𝖆𝖘 𝕵𝖊𝖋𝖋𝖊𝖗𝖘𝖔𝖓?

Quite possibly no one articulated Jefferson's gift of limitless natural intelligence better than President John F. Kennedy. While at a dinner at the White House on April 29, 1962, in honor of the forty-nine Nobel Prize winners sitting before him, the young and charismatic thirty-fifth president observed:

> I think this is the most extraordinary collection of talent, of human knowledge, that has ever been gathered together at the White House, with the possible exception of when Thomas Jefferson dined alone.[13]

Exactly. Drop the mic and close the curtains.

"Brilliance" must be *proven* and never *assigned*.

Imagine the reaction of the President Kennedy of 1962 to learn that the Patriot and president he so deeply admired had now become the *enemy* of so many from the Left. Imagine the reaction of that President Kennedy to the calls to tear down statues of Jefferson—*as done in New York City*—to sandblast his name off buildings and monuments, to smear his reputation, and to ultimately banish his name and accomplishments from the history of the very Republic he risked all to help create and grow.

I can and will only speak for myself. But I believe President Kennedy would have been repulsed and sickened by such vile tactics that have been employed in numerous totalitarian regimes throughout history.

The United States of today *is now* being battered by a totalitarian groupthink storm of epic proportions. One in which, sadly, those with the means and opposed to such suicidal groupthink have created no safe harbors of refuge from the ideological tsunami washing over and weakening every square inch of our nation.

The coming decade will tell the story of whether the Republic **Thomas Jefferson** and the other **55 Signers** gave all to create will in fact literally survive or be swept into the dustbin held in the cold, bony hand of tyranny.

But…once again, I digress.

✧

With regard to **Thomas Jefferson**—and given the never-ending attacks and accusations his name elicits today from many on the Left—it may be appropriate to start with some of the more personal and human details of his extraordinary life.

A quick summary of those follows.

Jefferson was born on **April 13, 1743,** in Goochland County, Virginia. He was the firstborn for Peter Jefferson and his wife, Jane Randolph Jefferson.

Tragically, Jefferson's father passed away when Jefferson was just fourteen years of age. What made matters much worse was by the time Peter Jefferson passed, he and his wife had eight children.

So suddenly, at fourteen years of age, Jefferson had to take on the responsibility of caring for his mother and seven siblings. More than that, he had to figure out how to manage the approximately 2,500 acres of land and farmland his father had left the family.

Two years later—after already proving himself to be an incredibly advanced student and intellect—he entered the College of William and Mary. Jefferson not only graduated from the then-acclaimed institution of higher learning in **1762,** but through posterity he also became its most famous and accomplished student.

*Or not...*if you happen to be a Far Left faculty member or student from *today's failing version* of the College of William and Mary and much of your day is filled with raging against the man who not only drafted the greatest document known to humankind but also went on to personify the terms Renaissance man, philosopher, scientist, inventor, politician, diplomat, musician, agronomist, and, most of all, humanitarian.

Fortunately for those who do share President Kennedy's opinion of Jefferson and who do believe he and his fellow **55 Signers** did give birth to the greatest nation the world has ever known, some 260 years before the ignorant leftist haters from William and Mary conspired to cancel him, **Thomas Jefferson** was hard at work growing into the man who would indeed change the world for the better.

Again, the acrimony and outright hate directed at Jefferson—and a number of other Founding Fathers—from many on the Left has been generated by their often selective country and worldview regarding the subject of slavery.

Also, again, it cannot be stressed enough how abhorrent and contemptible the practice of slavery was then or is today. It was and will always remain a crime against humanity.

Of course, if some on the Left and some in "big tech" do choose to ignore the slavery, forced-labor camps, and genocide taking place in certain other countries of *today*, I am sure *it has nothing to do with the money being generated for them in those countries.*

So much simpler to ignore the atrocities of today and go back over 250 years to single out certain **Founding Fathers** of our Republic to make examples out of them.

Can there ever be an excuse for slavery? *Never.*

Clearly those who were deeply troubled by the repugnant practice—Jefferson included—knew it was wrong across the very spectrum of humanity and yet still participated in it in one form or another.

As stated, that was a marker of infamy Jefferson wore for the rest of his natural life.

But with that very subject in mind, it would certainly be *fair*—and incredibly informative—if those on the Left who continually attack Jefferson and other **Founding Fathers** over the obscene practice of slavery also listed—in *great detail*—those in *today's world* engaged in the same repulsive practice and the corporations that profit from such slavery. Next, they could tell us what actions *they plan to take* against those nations and corporations to help eradicate such inhumanity.

It is clearly very easy for some to preach how it should have been…*then*. After all, if the Left of today is *certain* what was in the minds, hearts, and souls of those from over 250 years ago, then ascertaining the same information for those behind the slave camps, torture, and genocide of *today* should be mere child's play for them.

෴

In the meantime, going back over 250 years ago, we also learn that in January 1772, at twenty-eight years of age, Thomas Jefferson married Martha Skelton. The then-widowed Mrs. Skelton was twenty-three years of age and had inherited a tidy sum of money for the time.

Together, Jefferson and Martha shared the joy of bringing six children into the world. Tragically, together as a couple they also shared the unbearable grief of having to bury four of those children, as only two of the six lived to see adulthood.

Such were the times back then. Even for those from the "upper class" of the colonies.

All of that is to say that, by the time Thomas Jefferson had reached his early thirties, he had experienced a great deal of personal heartache and tragedy. Hard, grief-inducing lessons that were imbedded in his mind during those times necessitated that he had to switch mental gears to participate in the creation of a new Republic. Lessons that taught him that the liberty and happiness of a people was everything.

That noted, what follows are just *some* of the particulars of his remarkable career and unassailable genius.

Thomas Jefferson was elected to the House of Burgesses (the representative assembly for Colonial Virginia) in 1769. In 1775, he was elected to the **Continental Congress**.

But it was in between those years—1774 to be precise—that Jefferson authored what many believe to be the practice run for the **Declaration of Independence**.

It was a revolutionary and indeed radical pamphlet titled *A Summary View of the Rights of British America—Set forth is some Resolutions intended for the Inspection of the present Delegates of the People of Virginia now in Convention by a Member of the House of Burgesses—Williamsburg: Printed by Clementina Rind.*

Initially, as for the reasons mentioned regarding the resolution put forth by **Richard Henry Lee**, the author of this pamphlet was to be kept anonymous for his own safety. That said, when **Thomas Jefferson** received his printed copy of the pamphlet he himself wrote, he signed just under the notation for the House of Burgesses "by **Thomas Jefferson**."

Thanks to technology and the Library of Congress—a huge Jefferson connection there—you can view Jefferson's very own personal copy online, "turn" the pages, and read the entire text—*including his handwritten edits and corrections*—word for word. Not only is it quite remarkable, but every citizen of our Republic of today so able should do precisely that. It is a true portal back to 1774 and the literal mindset of Jefferson at that time.

As described by the Library of Congress:

> The pamphlet is Thomas Jefferson's personal copy of *A Summary View of the Rights of British America*, which he originally drafted in July 1774 as a set of instructions for the Virginia

delegates to the first Continental Congress. Jefferson argued that the British Parliament had no rights to govern the colonies, which he claimed had been independent since their founding. He also described the usurpations of power and deviations from law committed by King George III and Parliament. Jefferson was not present in the Virginia House when his draft instructions were debated and the House adopted a more moderate position than the one he articulated, but his friends had his instructions published in pamphlet form. The pamphlet was circulated in London, as well as in Philadelphia and New York, and helped to establish Jefferson's reputation as a skillful, if radical, political writer.[14]

"Radical."

Well, as has been said: *"One person's Radical is another's Founding Father."*

As noted in the section on **Richard Henry Lee**, Jefferson was not only appointed to the Committee of Five to draft the Declaration but also was tasked—based on his continually proven writing skills, most especially evidenced in *A Summary View of the Rights of British America*—with personally authoring the first draft of the document.

Next, with regard to Jefferson, we come to one of the greatest résumés in the history of our nation and, indeed, the world.

From 1779 until 1781, Jefferson served as the governor of Virginia. After taking just over three years off from serving the people to attend to his own private life, Jefferson returned to the public square and soon succeeded **Benjamin Franklin** as the minister to France in 1785, where he remained until October 1789. While in France, Jefferson became a symbol of intelligence, class, and, most of all, liberty to the literati of that nation who were advocating for more freedom for their own people.

Upon Jefferson's return to the United States, the newly minted first president of our Republic, **George Washington**, asked Jefferson to serve as the very first secretary of state.

In 1797, Jefferson was elected vice president of the United States. It should be noted that, at that time, the candidate getting the second most votes, was elected vice president.

With **John Adams** as president, Jefferson served in the role of vice president until 1801.

In 1801, Jefferson was elected our nation's third president, a title he held for two terms until 1809. During that time, among a number of other amazing accomplishments, he created the blueprints for the westward expansion of the Republic with the Louisiana Purchase—those 823,000 square miles instantly doubling the size of the United States—while also ordering the Lewis and Clark Expedition.

Again, given the significance of the titles held and *the timing of those jobs*, it's a résumé that stands alone for its time.

જ

Now, to close the section on **Thomas Jefferson**, after leaving the White House in 1809, he retired to his beloved Monticello home in Virginia to, among other things, establish the University of Virginia at Charlottesville. A place where today—*surprise, surprise*—many of the Far Left faculty and students are seeking to have his very name and legacy removed.

It was during Jefferson's post-presidency life at Monticello that the connection to the Library of Congress was established.

Toward the end of his life, Jefferson had, quite sadly, basically run out of the money needed to provide for himself, his family, and his home. Horrified and embarrassed by that development, a number of supporters of Jefferson worked with him behind the scenes to have Congress buy his very extensive library, a library that became the very foundation for...*the Library of Congress*.

And finally, to circle back to his connection to the second president of the United States, quite remarkably, both **Thomas Jefferson** and **John Adams** passed away exactly on the fiftieth anniversary of the **Declaration of Independence** on **July 4, 1826.**

Jefferson was eighty-three years of age.

CHAPTER SIX

John Hancock

Next on our list of the first seven to be highlighted for their critical roles in giving birth to the **Declaration of Independence**, we come to **John Hancock**.

Now, "Why," you might logically ask, "does Hancock come before the likes of **John Adams** and **Benjamin Franklin**?"

Primarily, because he was the *very first* to sign that founding document. That, in and of itself, rates very serious recognition.

Of course, he was the first to sign because he was, in fact, the president of the **Second Continental Congress**.

With regard to the most famous signature in recorded history, Hancock's duty as president of that congress does explain why he was the first to sign. But, a better question that persists to this day is "*Why* did he sign his name so large and so flamboyantly?"

Folklore and legend tell us that he did it so that the "fat old King (George III) could read it without his spectacles."[15]

A different version of that same folklore recounts that after signing his name in such a massive font, Hancock declared: "There. John Bull [a disparaging colonial nickname for Great

Britain] can read my name without spectacles and may double his reward on my head."

While a number of "experts" of today are quick to discount those reasons, as stated, it's never a wise move to pretend or assume to know what was in the mind, heart, and soul of someone centuries before.

The main reason in this case is that **John Hancock** for sure understood that the very second he signed his name to the **Declaration of Independence**, he was, in reality, signing his own death warrant.

And yet, knowing that to be a certainty, Hancock still signed his name in an oversized and ostentatious manner. This act of pure, unbridled defiance would come as absolutely no surprise to those who truly knew the "British antagonist" from Boston.

While the reasons why Hancock signed his name in such a large and "come get me" manner may be up for debate, a critically important fact regarding his signing is not.

To this very day, many Americans believe or assume that all **56 Signers** affixed their names to that **Declaration of Independence** on that same day—which just happened to be **July 4, 1776**.

Those beliefs and assumptions are flat-out incorrect.

The absolute fact of the matter is that on **July 4, 1776**, only one man signed the **Declaration of Independence**. Only one. That one being **John Hancock**. Yet another reason he should be so high on the list of those above equals when it does come to the **56 Signers**.

Of course, a large part of what caused so many Americans over the decades to have that wrong belief or make that wrong assumption is the very famous painting by John Trumbull commissioned in 1817, purchased in 1819, and placed in the

Capitol Rotunda in 1826. A painting Trumbull himself titled "𝕯𝖊𝖈𝖑𝖆𝖗𝖆𝖙𝖎𝖔𝖓 𝖔𝖋 𝕴𝖓𝖉𝖊𝖕𝖊𝖓𝖉𝖊𝖓𝖈𝖊, 𝕵𝖚𝖑𝖞 𝟦, 1776."

The painting, further made famous on the back of the two-dollar bill and bicentennial stamps, depicts the Committee of Five—𝕿𝖍𝖔𝖒𝖆𝖘 𝕵𝖊𝖋𝖋𝖊𝖗𝖘𝖔𝖓, 𝕭𝖊𝖓𝖏𝖆𝖒𝖎𝖓 𝕱𝖗𝖆𝖓𝖐𝖑𝖎𝖓, 𝕵𝖔𝖍𝖓 𝕬𝖉𝖆𝖒𝖘, 𝕽𝖔𝖌𝖊𝖗 𝕾𝖍𝖊𝖗𝖒𝖆𝖓, and 𝕽𝖔𝖇𝖊𝖗𝖙 𝕷𝖎𝖛𝖎𝖓𝖌𝖘𝖙𝖔𝖓—standing before 𝕵𝖔𝖍𝖓 𝕳𝖆𝖓𝖈𝖔𝖈𝖐.

The remaining men in one of our Republic's most famous paintings were the additional forty-one signers or other Patriots depicted by Trumbull as being present at what is now known as Independence Hall, Philadelphia.

Except…only 𝕵𝖔𝖍𝖓 𝕳𝖆𝖓𝖈𝖔𝖈𝖐 signed that document on 𝕵𝖚𝖑𝖞 𝟦, 1776.

Most of the remaining 𝟝𝟝 𝕾𝖎𝖌𝖓𝖊𝖗𝖘 added their signatures to the document on 𝕬𝖚𝖌𝖚𝖘𝖙 𝟤, 1776, with the last signature being secured in late November of that year.

One of the main reasons it took some longer than others to sign was because—as stated about Hancock—they knew that by doing so, they were also signing their own death warrants. For that reason, some of the signers hesitated out of understandable fear or because they wanted to get their affairs in order, or both.

But no matter the spin of today or what certain "experts" proclaim, the unconditional truth was that on 𝕵𝖚𝖑𝖞 𝟦, 1776, one man, and one man alone, courageously and defiantly signed that document as large, as clear, and as attention-getting as possible, and then sent it out to the world.

That man was 𝕵𝖔𝖍𝖓 𝕳𝖆𝖓𝖈𝖔𝖈𝖐.

Hancock was born in the then-village of Quincy, Massachusetts, in 1737. Hancock's father was a minister who passed away when Hancock was a small child. The father's passing caused immediate turmoil and financial problems for the family, as the home they were living in was dedicated to the minister in residence; as a new minister was about to move in to replace Hancock's father, forcing Hancock's mother to move out and split up her children to protect and care for them.

She took two of her children to live with their grandfather in Lexington, Massachusetts, while she sent her small child, John, to live with his massively wealthy uncle Thomas in the Beacon Hill section of Boston.

Hancock's uncle Thomas and his aunt Lydia had no children of their own and quickly came to love and care for young John as their own child. Because of his uncle's great wealth, young **John Hancock** wanted for nothing and was given everything. Included in that largesse by his uncle and aunt was a Harvard education.

Upon graduation, Hancock went to work for his uncle Thomas. As part of that job, in 1760 his uncle sent young Hancock on a business trip to London. Quite remarkably, and in an ironic twist of fate, while he was there he witnessed not only the funeral for King George II but also the coronation ceremony for *King George III*...the ruler whose edicts would soon put Hancock's life, and the very future of the colonies, at great risk.

Soon after Hancock's return to Boston, his uncle passed away and left his entire fortune to his nephew. Suddenly, at twenty-six years of age, he became, if not the wealthiest person in all of Boston and Massachusetts, very near the top and would have been considered a billionaire by today's standards.

To say that Hancock enjoyed his newfound station in life and great wealth might be an understatement. He most certainly did and almost immediately adopted a very lavish lifestyle.

But with that lifestyle came a burning contradiction from within him. Again, almost all the elites of that time were either Loyalists to the Crown or were, at the very least, sympathizers in the sense that they didn't want to say or do *anything* that might "rock the boat" holding their great fortunes.

From the moment he entered adulthood, Hancock viewed the Crown as an ever- oppressive and growing threat to the colonies. Most especially—and most certainly counterintuitively for many, considering his great wealth and station in life—he viewed the dictates of King George III and Great Britain as increasingly detrimental to *the poorest, working-class masses* within the colonies.

So now, if you will, we come to a hopefully fun comparison that fans of the *original Batman* comic book—first introduced in 1939 by Bob Kane and Bill Finger—may appreciate. Long before political correctness and "wokeness" eroded, compromised, and ruined that once great franchise, the young artists Kane and Finger introduced their title character as "*a mysterious and adventurous figure fighting for righteousness and apprehending the wrong doer, in his lone battle against the evil forces of society...*" in the guise of the ultrawealthy heir and "*socialite Bruce Wayne.*"

In that original 1939—now iconic—comic book introducing "The Batman," fictional Police Commissioner Gordon describes the wealthy young heir as:

> Bruce Wayne is a nice young chap, but he certainly must lead a boring life...seems disinterested in everything.

Again, just making a light point, but within that point, it is then at least entertaining to observe that **John Hancock** was *Bruce Wayne* centuries before Bruce Wayne and *Batman* ever existed. That being a seemingly "*disinterested chap*" trying to also do great good with the massive wealth he had inherited upon the passing of his father figure.

The fact that Hancock's uncle was named Thomas as was the father of the fictional Bruce Wayne is just a coincidence...*or is it?*

Okay, now back to Hancock's actual life before I offend any self-anointed purists for melding a bit of fact and fiction to make a relevant point.

That greater and relevant point is that **John Hancock** truly did enjoy his money and lived his life to the fullest. In his late twenties and early thirties Hancock was the talk of Boston precisely because of the extravagant parties he gave, the richly impeccable clothes he wore, and the mansion he inhabited on Beacon Hill.

But during those same years, he continually donated great sums of money to help Bostonians and others in need. So much so that he became just as well known for those acts of kindness and generosity as he was for his unrivaled wealth.

While Boston was arguably the most sophisticated and educated of the cities in then- colonial America, it was still a very small town in so many other ways. Chief among them was that some people were publicly willing to make their contempt for the Crown known.

John Hancock was just such a person, and because it was a small town in that sense and because many of the wealthy residents were committed Loyalists, Hancock's increasingly anti-Crown comments were loudly counterintuitive and soon came to the attention of one Samuel Adams.

As he was a signer of the Declaration, we will get into the life and background of Samuel Adams more fully in the coming pages, but for now, suffice it to say that many in Boston and eventually around the colonies considered him one of the true "fathers of the Revolution."

While Adams was also born into some degree of wealth and, like Hancock, went to Harvard, from adulthood his mind was filled only with politics and fighting the oppressions of Great Britain.

As he was fifteen years older than Hancock and the "senior citizen" of Boston's anti-Britain contingent, he soon found and took the openly vocal Hancock under his revolutionary wing.

Interestingly, while the older Adams did indeed become the political and revolutionary mentor to Hancock, it was the much younger Hancock who became at the time the financial protector of Adams by covering a number of his business and financial miscues.

In 1774, Hancock was elected as the president of the Provincial Congress of Massachusetts, an assembly that held its meetings in Concord.

By this time, both Hancock and his political mentor Samuel Adams were becoming serious thorns in the side of the British military governor, Thomas Gage. No mere politician, Gage was in fact a highly decorated military general who before becoming the military governor overseeing Massachusetts commanded all British military forces in North America.

As military commander—a posting he was given in 1763, which was headquartered in New York—he was in charge of a massive British military force with over fifty garrisons and outposts that spanned each direction from Newfoundland to Florida and from Bermuda to the Mississippi.

When it came to the colonies and their first hints of defiance, many considered Gage to be a brutal and unforgiving autocrat.

They were not wrong.

By 1774, General Gage had been transferred to Massachusetts to become its military governor. By the time of his arrival, he was already outraged by the 𝕭𝖔𝖘𝖙𝖔𝖓 𝕿𝖊𝖆 𝕻𝖆𝖗𝖙𝖞 𝖔𝖋 𝟣𝟩𝟩𝟥 and the nerve of some of the colonists to dare to want their own independence.

As such, his mental position against them had hardened considerably by that time. As we would say today, "The colonists were starting to live rent-free in the mind of Gage," as he became more and more angered and consumed by their "insolence."

Because of that, he began to send incendiary reports back to London on a regular and much more disturbed basis. These reports naturally further inflamed the Crown against the colonies.

More than that, Gage became the main instrument in causing the Crown's retaliatory Intolerable (Coercive) Acts of 1774, in which the port of Boston was blockaded as reprisal for the 𝕭𝖔𝖘𝖙𝖔𝖓 𝕿𝖊𝖆 𝕻𝖆𝖗𝖙𝖞.

More insidiously, Gage was also the one behind the hated and provocative provision calling for the headquartering of British soldiers in the homes of private citizens as well the dictatorial law ordering that *all* colonial democratic institutions were *superseded* by British military rule.

His rule.

It was in this mindset and with that rule in place that Gage decided he had had enough of the colonial upstarts—most especially, John Hancock and Samuel Adams.

In the guise of uncovering ammunition caches, he ordered his troops to march on Lexington and Concord. Again, while he would have been thrilled to locate and confiscate any ammunition or colonial supplies found, his main purpose was to capture those two men.

Little did Gage realize that he was about to personally start the American Revolution with his spiteful and provocative act.

By the time the British forces arrived in Lexington on April 18, 1775, the Massachusetts Minutemen had already been activated, and Hancock and Adams had been warned that they were the direct targets of an enraged General Gage, tipped off no less by the famous ride of Paul Revere.

As has been reported, as the redcoats entered the front door of the house Hancock and Adams were hiding, the two targets simultaneously escaped out the back door with their very lives.

Should anyone doubt the fate that would have befallen Hancock and Adams had they been caught, they need only take in the words of General Gage himself.

Following those history-making and -changing battles at Lexington and Concord, come June 12, 1775, General Gage decided to throw a few crumbs to the peasants and issued a proclamation offering pardons to all the rebels.

All the rebels except...*two*. Those being John Hancock and Samuel Adams.

With regard to the two Patriots who were eating away at his mind with their constant public outbursts favoring revolution, Gage stressed that all rebels would get pardons except Hancock and Adams: *"Whose offences are of too flagitious a nature to admit of any other consideration than that of condign punishment."*[16]

"Condign punishment" being the polite and elite way to say: *"Put to death by the most torturous means at our disposal."*

࿈

Death threats against him or not, Hancock became a man on a mission. There was no task, no favor, no donation, big or small, that he would not see to if the end result would be to further educate the people of the colonies on the need for independence while at the same time antagonizing the Crown.

In between all the rabble-rousing and "man about Boston" lavish lifestyle, in 1775, at thirty-eight years of age, Hancock fell in love and married Dorothy Quincy (1747–1830), the daughter of a Boston merchant and magistrate. While the couple was soon blessed with both a boy and a girl, as was tragically common for the time, neither child survived to reach adulthood.

Some have speculated that the loss of his children further forced Hancock's mind to focus all its attention on the fight for independence as a way to deal with and forget his grief.

While that may be true—and quite understandable—the fact is that he had plenty of fight within him before he and his wife suffered those losses.

That fight was evidenced by his actions supporting the **Boston Tea Party**, the public address he gave commemorating the **Boston Massacre**, and his very slick and calculated move in 1768 to purposely try to smuggle in a shipment of wine into Boston Harbor aboard his sloop—named the *Liberty*—to avoid paying tax to the British.

While the ship was stopped and it and its contents were permanently confiscated by the Crown, word of the "in your face" move by Hancock soon swept through Boston and the surrounding countryside, further elevating his folk-hero status as a man of means "in it for the people."

Because of his great wealth and larger-than-life lifestyle, many people wrongfully assumed that Hancock was only a force behind the scenes. Nothing could be further from the truth.

This truth tells us that, despite his almost unrivaled wealth, he was still desperate to be named the commander of the Continental Army. When the Congress chose 𝔊𝔢𝔬𝔯𝔤𝔢 𝔚𝔞𝔰𝔥𝔦𝔫𝔤𝔱𝔬𝔫 instead, Hancock was personally devastated.

But as he demonstrated time and again during those fateful years, he quickly put his disappointment aside and then proceeded to use almost all his remaining personal fortune to help fund that army while influencing others to follow his lead.

In 1777, Hancock resigned as the president of the Continental Congress and soon created an opportunity to lead at least a small army. That transpired when a contingent of some five thousand soldiers from Massachusetts gathered together in an attempt to recapture Newport, Rhode Island, from the British. While the attempt ultimately failed, the fact that Hancock tried to pull it off further ingratiated him into the hearts and minds of the people.

Hancock may have been an "elite Boston Brahmin," but to the people in and around Boston, he was a "swashbuckler," always willing to put it on the line no matter the cost to him.

Precisely because of that reputation, he was resoundingly elected the first governor of Massachusetts in 1780, a title he held when he passed away on October 8, 1793, at but fifty-six years of age.

All of Boston wept with the passing of their "Son of Liberty" and enduring hero.

CHAPTER SEVEN

Benjamin Franklin

Next on our list of the first seven, we come to **Benjamin Franklin**. We do so because, again, at least for this particular exercise, Franklin comes next in the order of the first seven who were most responsible for bringing the **Declaration of Independence** to life.

And what a life *he* led to help give birth to our most famous document.

During his formative years in the colonies and in Europe, and for well over a century later, **Benjamin Franklin** was literally and rightfully considered to be one of the greatest men who ever lived. Period.

Before getting into his Revolutionary years, what follows is a brief snapshot of just some of his accomplishments during that remarkable life.

He was a multidimensional businessman, a printer, an author, a scientist, a politician, a diplomat, an inventor, a scholar, and a philanthropist.

If **Thomas Jefferson** was a true Renaissance man—and he surely was—then **Benjamin Franklin**—who among many other things, invented the Franklin stove, lightning rod, and bifocal glasses—was a poor man's Renaissance man...on *steroids*.

And yet, it is these giants of American history—and others—whom many on the Left seek to cancel...forever.

Maybe precisely because they *don't teach* American history—or *honest* American history—in our schools anymore, these—usually—privileged and entitled students simply don't know and therefore no longer care about the history- and life-altering accomplishments of Franklin, Jefferson, and many of our other Founding Fathers.

And yet, they *should* know. And they *should* care. Because it is remarkable examples such as Franklin and Jefferson who could very well be role models for today's students trying to understand and navigate an increasingly uncertain, troubled, and dangerous world.

Of course, one of the first lessons Franklin and Jefferson might teach these students and their compromised professors is that *one of the reasons* the world in now so uncertain, troubled, and dangerous is because the media, academia, big tech, entertainment, science, and medicine are dominated by *only one ideology*. As documented from the beginning of recorded time, such domination always serves as a doorway to draconian dictates, destruction, and the eventual suicide of that group or civilization.

Were it possible, Franklin and Jefferson might tell these students that they morphed into the 𝔉ounding 𝔉athers we know today *precisely because* they felt it critically important to fight a totalitarian, one-sided groupthink mentality that was deciding and dictating how the masses should live *then* while meting out severe punishment to those who would dare to choose individual liberty over the Crown's imperial pronouncements.

This scenario should seem quite familiar to some of these entitled students should they pause for just a moment to look out from their $50k per year "elite" colleges, their gated communities, the windows of their Land Rovers, or, more importantly, from their anarchist behavior in the streets of our cities, which is robbing small—often minority—business owners of their livelihoods.

Naturally, Hell will freeze over long before the liberal, "highly educated" intelligentsia *ever* admit they were and are wrong or that their actions are destroying our nation along with *their* futures as well as the futures for *their* children and grandchildren.

But maybe that explains *why* Benjamin Franklin was *so* intelligent.

Maybe the key to Franklin's brilliance—once again *earned* and *never* assigned—was that he was so formally *"uneducated."*

While Franklin went on to become a huge benefactor of higher education—when it actually *meant something*—he himself chose to go to the "University of Hard Knocks and Real Life."

Real-life experience almost always trumps academics. Most especially if it is being taught by pretentious professors who have never once worked or once succeeded in the very fields they feign expertise.

To that point, we have a fun—*but spot-on*—example of this "highly educated ignorance" from the movie *Back to School*, which starred Rodney Dangerfield.

In the 1986 hit, Dangerfield's character, Thornton Melon, is a tough, streetwise, "uneducated," mega-successful, and wealthy CEO who enrolls as a freshman at a prestigious college to keep an eye on his featherweight of a son.

As the movie progresses, we find Dangerfield's character sitting in a business class with a tens of other students being taught by just such a pretentious professor with not one second of experience in the real world of business. What follows is an exchange between the Dangerfield character and that professor:

> Pretentious Professor: "There are two kinds of people in business today…the quick and the dead. So, rather than waste your time this semester…with a lot of useless theories…we're going to jump right in with both feet…and create a fictional company from the ground up. We'll construct our physical plant…we'll set up an efficient administrative…and executive structure…then we'll manufacture our product and market it. I think you'll find it very interesting and a lot of fun. So, let's start by looking at construction costs…of our new factory."
>
> Mr. Melon: "What's the product?"
>
> Pretentious Professor: "That is immaterial for the purposes of our discussion here…but if it makes you happy…let's say we're making tape recorders.
>
> Mr. Melon: "Tape recorders? Are you kidding? The Japanese will kill us on the labor costs."

Pretentious Professor: "OK, fine. Then let's just say they're widgets."

Mr. Melon: "What's a *widget*?"

Pretentious Professor: "It's a fictional product. It doesn't matter."

Mr. Melon: "Doesn't matter. Tell that to the *bank*."

Pretentious Professor: Ignoring Melon while turning to the blackboard: "On the board, you will see a cost analysis...for construction of a square-foot facility...which will encompass both factory and office space...and is fully serviced by all utilities...a railroad spur line and a four-bay shipping dock."

Mr. Melon: "Hold it, hold it. Why build? You're better off leasing...at a buck and a half a square foot. Take your down payment and put it into CDs...or something else you can roll over every couple of months..."

[*Some of Melon's fellow students now begin to turn toward him and take notes.*]

Pretentious Professor: "Thank you, Mr. Melon...but we'll be concentrating on finance...a little later in the term. For the time being, let's just concentrate on the construction figures, shall we? You'll see the final bottom line requires the factoring in of not just the material and construction costs, but also the architects' fees and the cost of land servicing."

Mr. Melon: "Oh, you left out a *bunch of stuff.*"

Pretentious Professor: "Oh, really? Like *what*, for instance?"

Mr. Melon: "First of all, you have to grease the local politicians for the sudden zoning problems that always come up. Then there's the kickbacks to the carpenters. And if you plan on using any cement in this building…I'm sure the teamsters would like to have a little chat with you…and that'll cost you. Then, don't forget a little something for the building inspectors. There's the long-term costs, such as waste disposal. I don't know if you're familiar with who runs that business…but I assure you it's not the boy scouts…"

[*Not surprisingly, now the entire class has turned toward Mr. Melon while furiously taking notes of every word he is speaking.*]

Pretentious Professor: "That will be quite enough, Mr. Melon. Maybe bribes and kickbacks and Mafia payoffs are how you do business but they are not part of the legitimate business world and they're certainly not part of anything I'm teaching in this class. Do I make myself clear? Now, notwithstanding Mr. Melon's input, the next question for us is *where* to build our factory."

Mr. Melon: "How about *Fantasyland*?"

Precisely, and why *the entire class rightfully erupts in laughter* realizing the real-world business ineptitude of the snobbish-pretentious professor.

❧

A good to great *real education* can be invaluable to not only the student, but also to those he or she will work for, advise, or lead for decades to come.

Obviously, the relative words in that sentence being "good" and "great." Again, measurements that are less and less attainable in today's politically correct and woke colleges and universities.

But, assuming one did get a "great" education, it can still be incredibly inferior in the absence of real-world experience.

Over the course of the last decade or so, our nation—and the American people themselves—has paid a tremendous price because a number of our political and intelligence "leaders" have either literally not worked one day in the real world or only a few months at best.

"Leaders" who—because of the "I know better than the little people" arrogance filling their minds *only* because they happened to attend Ivy League schools and then got brought into government by *equally entitled and ignorant* buddies—continually misread real-world situations and fail our nation dramatically in the process.

Benjamin Franklin was so *brilliant* precisely because his real-world experience taught him that not only did he *not know everything*, but also that there was much to learn, and he was desperate to experience as much of it as possible. His mind was the polar opposite of closed. It was an insatiable sponge soaking up the real and known world of his day.

To that point, years ago, I had a number of wonderful conversations with Apollo 11 Command Module pilot Michael Collins. Not only was he himself an exceptional writer, but he was an even better human being.

Back then, Mike told me a story of how soon after *he* was selected to become an astronaut for NASA, he was asked to be on the selection committee for the next group of astronauts. Back then, in pre-space shuttle days, there were no mission specialists, no nonpilots, and no astronauts picked because of diversity *over* real-world qualifications needed when actual lives were on the line.

Everyone fighting to get picked as a NASA astronaut in the mid-1960s was already the best of the best when it came to our nation's pilots. Back then, the workforce—NASA especially—*only* hired the best and the brightest. Today, only China and Russia have that survivalist mindset, and because they do, *tick, tick, tick* goes the clock as it winds down on U.S. domination of *anything*.

Mike and his colleagues had to pick a handful of future NASA astronauts from the cream of the crop. Knowing that, Mike told me they came up with a way to try and create a little separation from the very best of the best. That being to ask them questions about the rocket boosters they might soon fly atop and the spacecraft they might soon fly in, meaning the Saturn V and the Apollo Command Module.

Because, as Mike told me, "While they might be the best of the best when it comes to being test pilots and fighter pilots, they didn't know everything. No one does. And that may include what makes the Saturn V and the Command Module work."

With that in mind, Mike and his colleagues would then ask some fairly detailed questions about the spacecraft. Some of the "hair on fire, high-performance pilots" would try to finesse or even fake an answer rather than admit they didn't know.

"A few others," Mike said, "would openly and quickly answer, '*I don't know*, but I can't wait to learn all about it.' Every single time, we picked the guy who said, '*I don't know.*'"

Moral of that story: the smartest people in the world are *never afraid* to say: "I don't know." Conversely, some of the least intelligent, most insecure, and most dangerous people in the world will *never* say, "I don't know" or "I was wrong." Their egos, "education," and reputations within the elite cocktail circuit simply will never allow it.

"*Tick, tick, tick.*"

𝔅enjamin 𝔉ranklin helped to create the clock that marked the time of the birth of our Republic. Many from the Far Left, the pretentious elites, and those meekly sitting in the stands of the arena, wringing their hands in worry over the chaos transpiring before them, created the timer that will mark the implosion of what was once upon a time the greatest nation on the face of the Earth.

Now, back to the true genius that was 𝔅𝔢𝔫𝔧𝔞𝔪𝔦𝔫 𝔉𝔯𝔞𝔫𝔨𝔩𝔦𝔫.

He was born in my hometown of Boston—only one of the many reasons I am a bit partial to him, 𝔍𝔬𝔥𝔫 𝔥𝔞𝔫𝔠𝔬𝔠𝔨, and the other Bostonians—in 1706.

His father was a Puritan who emigrated from Great Britain in 1682. Without a real trade to fall upon in his new country, Franklin's father entered into the soap- and candle-making business more by happenstance than planning, and he remained in it for the rest of his life.

Because both of his parents were quite religious, they hoped that young Franklin would become a minister. When it became obvious to them that such a calling was not for their son, they abandoned the idea, with his father soon bringing him into his business full-time after just a hint of elementary education.

The word on the Boston streets of the day was that Franklin hated the candlemaking business and soon found himself working as a printer's assistant for his elder and very demanding brother, James.

In some ways, it was a match made in Heaven for Franklin. For even though his family's dire financial circumstances forced him to become a school dropout, he remained ever studious and his love for the written and printed word grew by the day. And now working at his brother's newspaper, the *New England Courant*, he was in a business that disseminated the printed word to the masses.

That was the good news. The bad news was that he had to constantly endure the often foul mood of his older brother. Quite ironically, part of the rift between the two brothers came about because of a clandestine scheme cooked up by the sixteen-year-old Benjamin.

As Franklin himself recounted in his autobiography:

> He (Franklin's brother, James) had some ingenious Men among his Friends who amuse'd themselves by writing little Pieces for this Paper, which gain'd it Credit, and made it more in Demand; and these Gentlemen often visited us. Hearing their Conversations, and their Accounts of the Approbation their Papers were receiv'd with, I was excited to try my Hand among them. But being still a Boy, and suspect that my Brother would object to printing any Thing of mine in his Paper, if he knew it to be mine, I contriv'd to disguise my Hand, and writing an anonymous Paper I put it in the Night under the Door of the Printing House.[17]

As prominently featured in the movie *National Treasure*, Franklin "disguised his hand" by writing letters to the paper under the name of Silence Dogood—a fictional widow of an equally fictional minister. As it turned out, the first letter was such a hit with the readers—brilliant and written with a cliffhanger, soap-opera flair—that Franklin penned thirteen more letters for the paper in the poor widow's name.

With regard to our *present problems* as a nation as the tentacles of socialism grown longer and stronger, it is worth noting what this "uneducated" sixteen-year-old boy wrote to close the second of his Silence Dogood letters to the *New England Courant* on **April 16, 1722**:

> Know then, That I am an Enemy to Vice, and a Friend to Vertue. I am one of an extensive Charity, and a great Forgiver of private Injuries: A hearty Lover of the Clergy and all good Men, and a mortal Enemy to arbitrary Government and unlimited Power. I am naturally very jealous for the Rights and Liberties of my Country; and the least appearance of an Incroachment on those invaluable Priviledges, is apt to make my Blood boil exceedingly [emphasis mine]. I have likewise a natural Inclination to observe and reprove the Faults of others, at which I have an excellent Faculty. I speak this by Way of Warning to all such whose Offences shall come under my Cognizance, for I never intend to wrap my Talent in a Napkin. To be brief; I am courteous and affable, good humour'd (unless I am first provok'd,) and handsome, and sometimes witty, but always, Sir, Your Friend and Humble Servant,
>
> SILENCE DOGOOD.

In 1722, a sixteen-year-old boy could see, fear, and cry out against that which our "leaders" of today either remain blind to or purposely ignore for personal gain and increased power.

The blood of us all should "*boil exceedingly*."

ॐ

Now, going back to 1722, many believed that James was already becoming envious of his clearly gifted younger brother. Once Benjamin admitted that it was indeed he who had written the Silence Dogood letters, which became the talk of Boston, the relationship between James and Benjamin further soured to the point where it became a hostile work environment for Benjamin.

Saddened and tired of the increasing put-downs and criticisms from his older brother, Franklin simply quit on the spot one day, walked down to Boston Harbor, and got on a ship heading to New York.

Once in New York, he could find no one willing to either employ him or give him shelter. While there, someone told him there was work and shelter to be found in Philadelphia.

So, at now just *seventeen years of age* and with but one dollar in his threadbare pants, Franklin headed *on foot* to Philadelphia.

As more and more of our young people stay at home—or in their parent's basements—and play video games while our ever-more socialist government sends them checks *not to work*, we really need to focus on what that seventeen-year-old boy did.

In order to find work and shelter, he literally *walked* from New York to Philadelphia—a city he arrived in some days later penniless and without knowing a single soul.

Gee, how could someone *with that kind of drive and belief in himself* ever go on to become one of our Founding Fathers?

Once in Philadelphia, Franklin made a beeline for the two major printers in the city and was immediately hired by one of them. Because of the relief, and joy, he felt at finding his dream job—for the moment—Franklin quickly excelled at it and was soon noticed and lauded by those in charge.

At this point, Franklin entered a bittersweet time period. Because of his tremendous work ethic and obvious intelligence, he found a benefactor in a prominent businessman who was willing to sponsor him. During that time, he also met a young woman with whom he soon fell in love. Her name was Deborah Read. Unfortunately for young Benjamin, while she liked him as a friend, she *loved* another man—a man she later married.

Because of this, when his business benefactor suggested Benjamin head to London to explore a business opportunity, Franklin jumped at the chance to, first, distract his mind from the heartache and, second, to visit and explore such an exciting and world-famous city.

After some time in London, while interacting with the best and even some of the worst the city had to offer, Franklin returned home to Philadelphia in July 1726 at the ripe old age of twenty.

Some four years later, Franklin's life took yet another fateful turn. The young woman he had fallen in love with, who had married another, was now a widow. After learning of this, Franklin once again reached out to Deborah Read Rogers. Soon after their courtship ensued, they married and consequently had two children, a daughter and a son. Sadly, their son was lost to smallpox at but four years of age.

Around this same time, Benjamin Franklin began to blossom into the intellectual, statesman and founder we revere today.

In 1730, he established and grew the *Philadelphia Gazette*, a newspaper that would become one of the most popular and influential in all of the colonies.

Three years later, Franklin created *Poor Richard's Almanack*. To be precise, he published the very first edition under the pseudonym Richard Saunders on December 19, 1732. That almanack would serve for the year 1733.

Like other almanacs of the time, Franklin's included information on the expected weather, important calendar dates, stories, sayings, poems, trivia, business, and a bit of gossip. What set *Poor Richard's Almanack* apart from the rest was Franklin's wit, style, humor, and gifted ability as a true storyteller. He had demonstrated these rare and in-demand skills approximately a decade before with his Silence Dogood letters.

Franklin's *Poor Richard's Almanack* became so popular across the land that he ended up publishing it once a year for the next quarter of a century—an endeavor that made him a great deal of money in the process.

In some ways, because of his financial success, he was better able to turn his amazingly brilliant mind to other interests that would prove to be for the better good of his fellow citizens.

These interests included the first public-lending library, the first fire department in Pennsylvania, and, as mentioned, numerous inventions with the goal of helping humanity.

During the Revolutionary War years, Franklin became part of the Continental Congress in May 1775; then more importantly he became one of the Committee of Five to help draft the Declaration of Independence, a document he would sign a few weeks later at seventy years of age as *the oldest Founding Father to do so*. Then, even more important in some eyes, Franklin was able to personally negotiate a Treaty of Alliance with France in 1778. This treaty brought that powerful nation in on the side of the colonies in the war for independence.

Five years later, Franklin traveled back to France, this time with John Adams and John Jay. Their mission? To sign the Treaty of Paris, which would bring an *official end* to the Revolutionary War.

Oh, and by the way to all the ignorant haters on the Left of the Founding Fathers, in 1787 Benjamin Franklin was elected as the first president for the Pennsylvania Society for Promoting the Abolition of Slavery—a fight he had committed himself to while still in his twenties.

Benjamin Franklin passed away in 1790 at eighty-four years of age.

CHAPTER EIGHT

John Adams

Next on the list of the first seven signers, we come to a name just mentioned in passing: John Adams.

What do you say about a Founding Father who was on the Committee of Five to help draft the Declaration of Independence; was instrumental in appointing George Washington as the commander of the Continental Army; was our first vice president; was our nation's second president; was the father of our nation's sixth president; and oh, by the way, had a storybook marriage, which in many ways, served as a true and accurate time portal into those Revolutionary War years?

Only as many superlatives as possible.

John Adams was born just outside of Boston—that "Cradle of Liberty"—on October 13, 1735. He was a direct descendant of the famous John Alden who came over on the *Mayflower*.

His primary education was attained in the then-Braintree area of Boston. By the age of twenty, he had graduated from Harvard College.

From there, he sought to establish himself in the practice of law. And while successful with that endeavor, there was something inside him that was not only eating away at him but also changing the way he viewed everyday life. That something was his revulsion to the oppressive and arbitrary "laws" being forced upon the people of the colonies by the uninformed and often cruel dictates of the Crown.

What to do?

Initially, Adams satisfied his growing resentment of the Crown by writing and publishing various criticisms of it and its policies in the local papers. Soon, those acts of defiance—which were anything but minor as they were identifying him publicly as a potential "enemy" of the Crown—grew hollow to Adams.

He felt the need to step up his activism and did so through the counsel and friendship of two prominent Bostonians. One was John Hancock; the other was his older——and increasingly more rabble-rousing—cousin, Samuel Adams.

After the British Parliament passed the hated Stamp Act on March 22, 1765—a punitive act against the colonists, which forced them to pay a tax on about every form of paper, documents, and even playing cards to subsidize the housing of the British troops in the colonies—Adams turned full-blown revolutionary in mindset.

For him, enough was enough, and there would be no going back.

Initially after that act, he did the only thing he could, which was to dial up his anti-Crown writings as a way to further fuel the colonists' resentment against the king and Parliament.

It was working.

So much so that the royal governor of that time, Francis Bernard, endeavored to buy the silence of Adams by offering him various offices as enticement. These offers were immediately rejected by a now-satisfied Adams, who knew that not only was he getting under the skin of the royal governor but also that his anti-Crown messages were making a real impact.

That said, to many of the colonists of the day—most especially in Boston—**John Adams** was a bit of an enigma or, even for a time, someone to be looked down upon and scorned. The reason for that was simple. Adams was a man who strongly believed that "right was right and wrong was wrong."

If he felt something was wrong or unfair, he would speak out against it. *No matter what.*

That strong belief and unbreakable principle was on full display on the morning of **March 6, 1770.** Just hours earlier a contingent of British redcoats had gunned down five colonists just outside the Boston Custom House in an act almost immediately dubbed the **Boston Massacre.**

The "facts"—at least as the biased Bostonians saw them—could not have been more clear. The colonists were innocent angels advocating for their rights, and the redcoats were vicious monsters who killed five colonists in cold blood.

Maybe. Maybe not.

One person who wanted to be sure was a then-thirty-four-year-old Boston lawyer by the name of **John Adams.** After doing a bit of his own investigative work, Adams came to believe that the British soldiers who fired on the colonists were truly in fear for their lives and took that last resort only to *protect* their lives.

Having come to that conclusion, Adams then did something truly unthinkable for that time. This proven anti-Crown Patriot and highly respected voice in Boston and the colonies decided it was his duty to…*defend* the British officer Thomas

Preston and his soldiers against the charge of murder. He commenced to do this almost to perfection in two separate trials.

But by doing so, Adams put not only his reputation and very livelihood at great risk but also his life and the lives of his family, as many in Boston were convinced of the guilt of those "British monsters."

A fitting parallel to that for today's times might be if say, a well-known liberal, Far-Left lawyer decided to defend a contingent of New York City, Chicago, or Boston police officers who fired against a mob of Far-Left anarchists who were rampaging and looting in the streets and then turned their unhinged rage on those police, who then fired as a last resort *only* to save their very lives.

While I seriously doubt there is *any* Far-Left lawyer out there today with the courage and principles of 𝕵𝕠𝕙𝕟 𝕬𝕕𝕒𝕞𝕤, it still serves as a relevant example.

Even though Adams grew more anti-Crown by the day, he also knew that something was very wrong with the myth already being spread about the 𝔅𝔬𝔰𝔱𝔬𝔫 𝔐𝔞𝔰𝔰𝔞𝔠𝔯𝔢 across the Massachusetts and the colonial countryside.

Adams knew that like any army of the time, most of the soldiers were in fact very young conscripts who were simply trying to survive and maybe send a little money home to their families in the process.

Adams also knew that some of his fellow Bostonians liked to get fired up, with their anger often being artificially fueled by alcohol from the local taverns—a recipe for disaster we see ad nauseam today.

While there was a great deal of confusion and "he said/she said" testimony during the two trials, it was the testimony of *one witness* Adams called that truly turned the tide in favor of the redcoats.

The testimony of Dr. John Jeffries, who had treated one of the mortally wounded colonists shot by the British soldiers, proved decisive. Just before the colonist passed away, he explicitly told the doctor that the British did indeed "fire upon us in self-defense."

Captain Preston and his men were found innocent by the Boston jury. While many in and around Boston truly did resent—or even hate—**John Adams** for a time after that trial, that resentment slowly turned to even greater respect because, in him, the colonists knew they had a defender of *them and their rights* of the highest order who would never give up the fight.

But while Adams was indeed a defender of innocent men, he was a fiercer advocate for the rights of the citizens of the colonies. Citizens he believed must be free from the onerous and destructive whims of the Crown.

Toward that end, in 1774 he was appointed to the First Continental Congress. Two years later, he was one of the most respected and sought-out members of the Second Continental Congress. In the congress he quite ferociously advocated for the resolution calling for complete independence from the Crown as advocated by **Richard Henry Lee**.

In many ways, because of the unflinching defense of that resolution laid forth by such a highly gifted orator and lawyer, his fellow delegates voted its acceptance. More than that, as mentioned, they picked Adams as one of the five in charge of drafting that actual **Declaration of Independence**, the final version of which was accepted and ratified on **July 4, 1776**.

Of interest, even though **John Hancock** had become a close friend and even mentor to Adams in a number of ways, Adams ultimately backed **George Washington** as commander of the Continental Army. Adams did this in spite of the fact that he was well aware that his good friend Hancock was actively seeking that command. It was said that things got a bit chilly between Adams and Hancock after that appointment, but both men soon moved on from it for the betterment of their friendship and the formidable task and years still before them.

Then, during and after the colonies' war for independence, **John Adams** served in Europe with great distinction. In 1777, he was named the special commissioner to the Court of France, a position previously held by **Benjamin Franklin**.

While in France and with side trips to London, Adams discovered that the position of the Crown was indeed hardening against the colonies and transmitted this finding back to the delegates of the Continental Congress. In addition to Adams helping to negotiate the Treaty of Paris, he also served as America's first ambassador to the Court of St James.

While all of that was impressive and truly laudatory, Adams deeply missed home and the people he had fought so hard to serve and protect.

But most especially, he missed his wife, Abigail.

Thankfully for us and those interested in honest history, it was precisely because Adams and his beloved wife were separated by a vast ocean for long stretches of a time that we have such clear window into the most important years regarding the birth of our Republic.

John and Abigail loved each other dearly and missed each other even more. Because of that, they exchanged hundreds of letters over those years. Today these letters serve as not only transcripts of the time but also as windows into some of the innermost thoughts of one of our most important and revered Founding Fathers.

Once home, in **1789** Adams became our nation's very first vice president. If some were to understandably believe that Adams would be overjoyed with such an honor, then they do not know him.

Again, he became vice president because at the time the candidate with the *second most* electoral votes was named to that position. Adams made clear he loathed the position when he wrote that the vice presidency was "*the most insignificant office that ever the invention of man contrived.*"[18]

Luckily for him and our infant nation, in **1797** he was elevated to the "most significant" office that ever the invention of man contrived: *president of the United States.*

During his time as both vice president and president, the debate about the proper role of the federal government was growing more heated between those who helped to create the new nation.

John Adams decided to align himself with the Federalists, who were led at the time by **Alexander Hamilton**. That decision put Adams squarely on the opposite side of the likes of **Thomas Jefferson** and **Richard Henry Lee**, who were troubled with so much power and authority being placed into one overarching and new government. Most especially since America had just won her independence from the all-powerful Crown.

All that debate and tension, coupled with his advancing age and the desire to spend more time with his family, helped to convince Adams that he wanted only one term as president before heading off into retirement from public life. So, in **1801**, after that one term, he did gracefully step off the public stage and dive back into his private life.

Sadly, some seventeen years later, he lost his dear Abigail when she passed after fifty-two years of marriage.

In spite of that loss, Adams was due one more amazing first and true moment of joy. That was when he lived to see his son, John Quincy Adams sworn in as our nation's sixth president in 1825.

Approximately one year later, on July 4, 1826—on exactly the fiftieth anniversary of the Declaration of Independence—John Adams passed away at the age of ninety. Quite ironically, it has been reported that his final words were "Thomas Jefferson still survives."

Little did Adams know that he and his great friend Jefferson were both going to meet their Maker on that same day at almost the exact same time—fifty years to the day after helping to create the greatest document known to humanity.

CHAPTER NINE

Robert R. Livingston

𝕬 s mentioned earlier, **Robert R. Livingston** was a member of the Committee of Five designated by the Continental Congress to draft the Declaration. He, along with **John Adams**, **Benjamin Franklin**, **Roger Sherman**, and most especially **Thomas Jefferson**, carried out that duty to perfection. Unfortunately, when the time came for him to sign the founding document he helped to create, Livingston was called back to New York on urgent business.

That said, being denied the honor of signing the Declaration did not stop Livingston from continually contributing to the literal creation of our nation.

One of Livingston's most significant contributions is usually attributed to another great American Patriot. Many of us were taught that **Thomas Jefferson** was responsible for the Louisiana Purchase, a negotiation and event that literally transformed the shape and future of the United States of America. And while Jefferson indeed deserves great credit, it was actually **Robert R. Livingston** who—while serving as the resident minister in the Court of Napoleon in Paris—engaged in the day-to-day negotiations that made the purchase possible.

But if helping to guide the drafting of the 𝔇eclaration of 𝔍ndependence and being the force behind the Louisiana Purchase are not impressive enough, maybe the next item on the agenda will check that box forever more. Livingston—in his role as the chancellor of New York (at the time, the highest judicial position in the state)—swore 𝔊eneral 𝔊eorge 𝔚ashington into office as the first president of the United States on 𝔄pril 30, 1789, as the war hero stood on the balcony of Federal Hall on Wall Street in New York City, which temporarily served at the first capital of our new Republic.

Of note, after that historic ceremony, it was soon decided that the capital would be relocated to Philadelphia in 1791 for a ten-year period. Once that decade was over, it would move once again to a stretch of farm and marshland personally selected by Washington—with input from 𝔗homas 𝔍efferson and 𝔄lexander 𝔥amilton—which encompassed lands from both Virginia and Maryland. This stretch would come to be known as Washington, DC.

As we were once taught, 𝔓ierre 𝔠harles 𝔏'𝔈nfant was chosen to design the "federal city" of the United States of America. By 𝔍une 1800, the new seat of power for our nation was up and running. A nation 𝔯obert 𝔯. 𝔏ivingston did serve at the highest of levels.

Livingston was born into wealth in New York City on 𝔑ovember 27, 1746. In his midteens, he attended and graduated from King's College (now Columbia University) in 1764.

Soon after graduation, he studied law under 𝔚illiam 𝔖mith, the then-chief justice of New York. With that exceptional training behind him, Livingston went on to become one of the most acclaimed lawyers in the colonies.

That profession was just one of his most prominent day-time jobs. At night, it was strongly rumored that he (and his brother, William) were very active leaders of the New York wing of the **Sons of Liberty**.

Whatever would the snobby aristocracy of New York have said about that mingling with the underclasses had they found out?

Going back to less controversial undertakings, the immensely impressive Livingston was also a member of the Provincial Congress of New York and, as highlighted, one of the key delegates to the Second Continental Congress.

Livingston was also appointed secretary of foreign affairs soon after the **Articles of Confederation** were adopted. He served in this position until 1783, when he was appointed chancellor of the State of New York.

In 1788, his was one of the loudest voices in support of the US Constitution, and he was able to serve as a delegate to the New York Convention, which ratified that document.

One year later came his swearing in of our first president.

A lesser-known but fun fact about Livingston—and one that made him even wealthier—was that he was a benefactor to the inventor Robert Fulton, the guy who gave birth to the steam engine, which led to the creation of steamboats—steamboats Livingston then helped to bring to New York while controlling much of the industry.

Robert R. Livingston passed away at sixty-six years of age on **February 26, 1813**. His was a life lived to the fullest to the benefit of a grateful nation.

Chapter Ten

Roger Sherman

The last of the seven who deserve to be mentioned first when speaking to the creation of the 𝔇eclaration of 𝔍ndependence is 𝔯oger 𝔖herman. Or, as he was lumped in with 𝔯obert 𝔏ivingston, the second of the "*two others*."

And just as with Livingston, *what* an "other." But, unlike Livingston, Sherman did get to sign the 𝔇eclaration of 𝔍ndependence.

He came to do so after independently following the blueprint of 𝔅enjamin 𝔉ranklin. Meaning that, like Franklin, 𝔯oger 𝔖herman was not only a self-made man but also a self-educated man with an insatiable appetite for learning.

Born in Newton, Massachusetts, on 𝔄pril 19, 1721, Sherman went about teaching himself everything he could possibly learn about great literature, the law, science, and the ever-more-powerful world of politics.

By the time he was about twenty-two years of age, he had relocated down to New Milford, Connecticut. Once there, simply by the coincidence of the creative, he followed even more deeply in the footsteps of Franklin.

Like Franklin, Sherman had a flair for writing and storytelling, and soon created his own very successful almanacs, which were read very widely in his area.

In 1754, this *self-educated* intellectual was admitted to the bar and practiced law for the next seven years. During that time, Sherman still somehow managed to find the time to become a justice of the peace, a county judge, and a local politician.

Still wanting to experience more out of life, Sherman shut down his successful law practice in 1764 and moved to New Haven so he could accept the position of treasurer of Yale College. Because the job was his for as long as he wanted it, most would have assumed that he would be content to settle into that role for the remainder of his working life.

Not Roger Sherman.

He not only became an associate judge of the Connecticut Supreme Court, but he was also appointed a delegate to the First and Second Continental Congresses. As if that were not enough—and it never was for Sherman, whose Patriotic roots ran as deep as his intellect—his fellow delegates at the Second Continental Congress knew that he was a man above in so many positive ways and, because of that, appointed him to that Committee of Five to draft the Declaration of Independence.

More than that, Sherman was also appointed to the committee to draft the Articles of Confederation.

As they used to say in the late, late-night ads: "But wait. There's more."

Sherman was also behind the drafting of what became known as the Great Compromise. This laid out a system in which the people of the new United States of America would be represented by a percentage of the population in the lower house but with equal representation in the upper house.

Talk about a remarkable career.

And just to cap it off, **Roger Sherman** was one of *only two men* who signed the three main founding documents of our nation: the **Declaration of Independence**, the **Articles of Confederation**, and the **Constitution of the United States of America**.

For over half a century, this self-made, self-educated man excelled at improving the lives of his fellow citizens. And in the process, he was a driving force behind the establishment of our nation.

Roger Sherman passed away in **1793** at the age of seventy-two.

CHAPTER ELEVEN

Samuel Adams

Now we come to...𝕿𝖍𝖊 𝕱𝖎𝖓𝖆𝖑 𝕱𝖎𝖋𝖙𝖞. While the following fifty 𝕱𝖔𝖚𝖓𝖉𝖎𝖓𝖌 𝕱𝖆𝖙𝖍𝖊𝖗𝖘 did indeed sign the Declaration of Independence and were truly remarkable men in their own right, I believe one man should come before the next forty-nine. That man is 𝕾𝖆𝖒𝖚𝖊𝖑 𝕬𝖉𝖆𝖒𝖘.

Again, just because I happen to come from the Dorchester neighborhood of Boston does not mean I'm trying to play favorites and single out the Boston guys, as in those 𝕱𝖔𝖚𝖓𝖉𝖎𝖓𝖌 𝕱𝖆𝖙𝖍𝖊𝖗𝖘 who just happen to come from the city known as "the Cradle of Liberty."

I'm simply trying to follow the history that, in this case, does once again lead right back to Boston. And later, it seems... an exceptional beer.

Speaking of 𝕾𝖆𝖒𝖚𝖊𝖑 𝕬𝖉𝖆𝖒𝖘 and beer, some snippets of biased history like to report that he was a ne'er-do-well or even a complete screwup who managed to bankrupt the brewery he inherited from his daddy.

Talk about disrespectful, ignorant, and completely missing the point of the man and the revolutionary Adams grew to be.

Instead of giving any credence to some of those ignorant or even deliberate potshots taken at **Samuel Adams**, let's instead view the opinion of one **Thomas Jefferson**.

Jefferson spoke often and highly of Adams, a Patriot he declared was *"truly the Man of the Revolution."*[19]

The media of that time went even further, stating among other platitudes that Adams was the "Father of the Revolution" and the "Father of American Independence."

Why?

It truly seems that **Samuel Adams** was preordained to become the leading revolutionary of the colonies.

Born in Boston on **September 22**, **1722**, Adams did enter the world in a protective bubble of wealth. His father was indeed a very successful businessman with several highly productive ventures, one being a brewery.

Because of his family's station in life among the upper crust of Boston, Adams, like a number of other **Founding Fathers** from that Cradle of Liberty, also attended and graduated from Harvard College.

Of important note, while at Harvard—*and still in his late teens*—Adams began his master's thesis on the justification of independence from and even revolution against... Great Britain.

Upon his graduation, it was his parents' wish that he enter the field of law. When they realized that was not going to happen, his father endeavored to fold him into the family businesses.

Again, to some, it does seem as if the path and the fate of **Samuel Adams** were chosen long before his birth—a path and a fate that did not include success in the business world, a world that held zero interest to Adams.

From his earliest adolescent years, Adams was fascinated by the politics of the day, as he knew it was politics, and the men involved with the politics, that controlled the levers of government, impacting every man, woman, and child within the colonies.

As a young teen in Boston, the exceedingly bright Adams understood that the people of the colonies needed to have complete control over those levers of power if they were to be in control of their own fate. To help make that need and hope a reality, Adams decided to dedicate any intellectual and organizational gifts to the cause of the rebellion.

To label **Samuel Adams** as the "Father of the Revolution" and a "mentor to the other **55 Signers**" would not be an overstatement. In fact, it would be spot-on accurate. He was those things and so much more.

However, before his political-Revolutionary time began, he experienced a great deal of the ups and downs of real life that impact every human being. In 1748, his wealthy father passed away. As Adams was the eldest child, he inherited the fortune.

In October 1749, he married Elizabeth Checkley, a reputed beauty who just happened to be the daughter of his pastor. In the next several years, Adams and his wife would have six children. Sadly, only two would live into adulthood. Even more tragically, in 1757, soon after giving birth to a stillborn child, Elizabeth herself passed away.

While Adams had become politically active about ten years earlier—first as a *lax* tax collector and then in the Massachusetts House—some felt that it was after losing his Elizabeth—much like other **Founding Fathers** who experienced such loss—that he poured his heart and soul into the movement as a way to distract from the constant grief.

And pour them in, he did.

In many ways—and most especially the early years before the Revolution—Adams had transformed himself into a one-man public relations machine against the rule of the Crown. He was relentless in the writing and publishing of letters in various newspapers in and around Boston denouncing the British "oppressors" in the most negative and colorful of terms. Included among those newspapers was a weekly he and some associates had started *only* to harass the British.

More than that, he very cleverly began to use various pseudonyms to sign his nonstop barrage of published letters, giving the impression to the colonists and British military leadership alike that there was a growing and fervent grassroots opposition to the rule of the Crown blossoming in the area.

Fearing that the public relations campaign would not be enough to stoke the fires of resistance within the colonists, Adams decided to up his game substantially and quite dramatically.

He did so by becoming the driving force behind the creation of the **Sons of Liberty**.

Now, while some have described the **Sons of Liberty** as everything from a "grassroots organization" to "instigators" to "provocateurs," the absolute fact of the matter was that the group was created in secret with but one purpose: to intimidate colonists loyal to the Crown and, most especially, to anger the British government and military by becoming a permanent thorn in its side.

In the summer of 1765 in Boston, an influential group calling themselves the "**Loyal Nine**," would meet regularly in pubs to discuss their options regarding opposition to the Crown. While not officially part of the **Loyal Nine**, two men behind the scenes greatly influenced that group: **Samuel Adams** and **John Hancock**.

By this time, Adams and Hancock had built an unbreakable friendship. While real, the friendship was also most certainly codependent at times.

Hancock saw Adams as a brilliant political tactician and street-level instigator who *was* the leading original voice against the Crown. But, with that reality, Hancock also knew that his friend could only excel in *that world* and never at business. And for that reason, as mentioned, Hancock was happy to bail Adams out of financial distress from time to time: charity given in true friendship and for the greater good of the cause.

Aside from helping Adams financially periodically, many believe that Hancock was also a secret and generous funder of the very secret **Sons of Liberty**.

While endeavoring not to be publicly tied to the group, both Adams and Hancock felt it essential to launch the **Sons of Liberty** as a way to continually undermine the rule of the Crown.

In a number of ways, they were more successful than they ever could have imagined when the need first dawned on them.

Initially, the **Sons** would meet under the cover of darkness beneath what was called the "Liberty Tree" in the Hanover Square Park in Boston. When not meeting there, they could again be found in various pubs in the area.

While their most famous act of "civil disobedience" was dumping 92,000 pounds of British tea into Boston Harbor in **December 1773** in what became known as the **Boston Tea Party,** the fact was that they had quickly grown into a powerful and even feared group long before that event.

Months after coming into being in the summer of 1765 as a way to initially protest the Stamp Act, the Sons had grown to over two thousand in number in just the greater Boston area alone.

With regard to that protest against the Stamp Act, Adams himself cleverly gave credit to the Sons of Liberty in an essay he wrote for the Boston Gazette. Proclaimed Adams in part:

> We cannot surely have forgot the accursed designs of a most detestable set of men, to destroy the Liberties of America as with one-blow, by the Stamp-Act; nor the noble and successful efforts we then made to divert the impending stroke of ruin aimed at ourselves and our posterity. The Sons of Liberty, on the 14th of August, 1765, a Day which ought to be forever remembered in America, animated with a zeal for their country then upon the brink of destruction, and resolved, at once to save her, or like Samson, to perish in the ruins, exerted themselves with such distinguished vigor, as made the House of Dogon to shake from its very foundation; and the hopes of the lords of the Philistines even while their hearts were merry, and when they were anticipating the joy of plundering this continent, were at that very time buried in the pit they had digged. The People shouted; and their shout was heard to the distant end of this Continent.

> In each Colony they deliberated and resolved,
> and every Stampman trembled; and swore by
> his Maker, that he would never execute a com-
> mission which he had so infamously received.[20]

Imagine that. A *Harvard man* in 1765 endeavoring to *pro-tect* the people while helping to create the greatest nation ever known compared to the legions of Harvard alumni in 2022 working as one to tear it down.

Now, going back to Adams in 1765, soon other secret chapters of the **Sons of Liberty** began springing up all over the colonies, most notably in New York and Virginia.

While intimidation against Loyalists and the Crown was most certainly an underlying tactic of the **Sons**, an even more powerful one was the publicity of the group and its grow-ing acts of civil disobedience and even insurrection *around* the colonies.

This was accomplished to *great success* because a number of the most influential members of this very secretive group were in fact local newspaper publishers and printers.

Starting in 1765, the **Sons of Liberty** had a very firm hand on the control of *the most important megaphone of their era*: the newspapers.

How important was that fact and how successful were the **Sons** in their never-ending campaign against British rule?

In a word: very.

By 1766, there were secret chapters of the **Sons** all over the colonies. So much so, that at least in the eyes of the colonists, they had come to *replace* the royal governors as the true source of power in the region. Governors had not only come to fear the **Sons** but also would often go into hiding to avoid them.

It is critically important to note that one of the reasons the **Sons** grew so fast and became so powerful and even feared was because they had created a secret chain of correspondence to regularly communicate with each other.

This chain of communication was suggested and refined by **Samuel Adams**. Why is that fact important?

Because **Samuel Adams** used that very same template to create the **Committees of Correspondence** later for all the colonies to formally communicate with each other. This tactic was also employed independently by the great **Richard Henry Lee**.

To close on the **Sons of Liberty**, with **Samuel Adams** and **John Hancock** helping to guide and fund a group that *did succeed* in inflaming the colonists against the Crown, is it any wonder, as mentioned earlier, that General Thomas Gage wanted the two men hunted down and severely punished?

To close this section on this truly remarkable man and the legitimate "Father of the Revolution," we have the following.

Adams was also one of the first to suggest the creation of the "Continental Congress," a body he then served from 1774 until 1781.

In 1793 the grateful people of Massachusetts elected Adams governor.

Samuel Adams wrote and spoke hundreds of thousands of words in the defense of the people and the need for a new nation free from oppression. Perhaps none so forcefully and eloquently sum up his courage and conviction as his words in 1774 when General Gage had sent an emissary to attempt to bribe the hated Adams to cease his hostilities toward the Crown. Said Adams in response to that futile attempt:

I trust I have long since made my peace with the King of Kings. No personal consideration shall induce me to abandon the righteous cause of my country. Tell Governor Gage, it is the advice of Samuel Adams to him, no longer to insult the feelings of an exasperated people.[21]

Magnificent.

Samuel Adams passed away in his beloved Boston on **October 3, 1803,** at eighty-two years of age.

CHAPTER TWELVE

Button Gwinnett

We now move on to the following **Forty-Nine** signers. From this amazing group of Patriots, we have tales of **Founding Fathers** being lost at sea, being shot and killed in a duel, being poisoned for money, arriving as indentured servants, being burned out of their homes, becoming prisoners of war; dying after being abused by their British captors, losing wives who were also abused by their Crown captors, losing sons in the war, bankrupting themselves to defeat the British, ending up in debtors prison, serving as an active clergyman, becoming involved in a secret cabal to remove George Washington from command, enduring multiple hand-to-hand battles, and ordering the Continental Army to fire upon his own home because the redcoats had taken it over.

Again, each and every one of the following **Forty-Nine Founding Fathers** was exceptional in his own way. That acknowledged, as this is a tome honoring them as well as the **Declaration of Independence**, they will be listed as they signed our most important founding document starting from the left-hand column and finishing with the right.

The first of the **Forty-Nine** is **Button Gwinnett**.

Aside from having arguably the most unique or even coolest name among the Founding Fathers, **Button Gwinnett** sadly became somewhat famous for the way he departed this Earth.

Gwinnett was born in Gloucestershire, England, around 1735. Upon reaching adulthood, he apprenticed as a merchant in Bristol before endeavoring to set up his own business. Around that same time, he married Ann Bourne.

As Gwinnett was struggling to establish his own business in England, he began to hear tale after tale from sailors returning to England from America of the promise of that new land and the potential treasures it held for an ambitious young man.

Allured by those tales, Gwinnet placed himself, his young wife, and possibly one daughter on a ship heading to the Americas. The ship deposited them at Charleston, South Carolina, in 1770.

Once there, he set up a one-man mercantile business. After approximately two years, he sold all his stock and used the money to purchase a large track of land on St. Catherine's Island in Georgia.

Unfortunately for Gwinnett, he had no experience as either a landowner or a farmer and soon sank into deep debt. For those reasons, his creditors took over his property but did allow him and his family to remain in their home.

During this time, he had also established a close friendship with fellow Georgian—and soon to be fellow signer of the **Declaration of Independence—Lyman Hall**. It is believed that numerous conversations with Hall brought Gwinnett into the Patriot cause.

While an unsuccessful farmer and businessman, Gwinnett was able to establish himself as both a justice of the peace and a member of the Georgia Colonial Assembly. From that foundation, he was elected to the Continental Congress.

On July 2, 1776, he voted for the Declaration of Independence and signed the actual document on August 2.

By this time, Mr. Gwinnett was coming into his own as not only a Patriot and Founding Father but also a leading voice for the future of Georgia. Unfortunately for him, it was soon after that high-water mark that life turned a bit more murky for him. This reality may have come about—or at least have been made worse—by his own hubris and snobbish beliefs.

Gwinnett truly had found his stride and was even instrumental in drafting a state constitution for Georgia as well as briefly serving as the governor of the colony in 1777 after the sudden death of Archibald Bulloch. But then, some feel he may have overreached with regard to his personal ambition and even his estimate of his own abilities to carry out his next desired duty.

With the winds of war blowing toward Georgia, Gwinnett also wanted to command the colony's militia. The command instead went to General Lachlan McIntosh, who was not only a seasoned soldier but also one who had already fought in multiple battles.

For reasons of his own, Gwinnett was highly insulted that the command went to McIntosh. Some of the earliest recounting of that history speculated that as a "native-born Englishman" Gwinnett felt himself—as so many did at the time—far superior to any man born in the colonies. Such snobbery may have been eating away at him as General McIntosh fell comfortably into his role.

At one point, Gwinnett and McIntosh argued over what to do with regard to the Loyalists living and hiding out in

Florida. The argument soon grew quite heated, and Gwinnett impulsively decided to challenge the battle-hardened general to a duel.

Mistake.

The general accepted the challenge, and they met early on the morning of May 16, 1777, to commence the duel. From a distance of twelve paces, each fired upon the other with pistols. Both men were instantly wounded—Gwinnett, as it turned out, fatally.

Button Gwinnett passed away three days later at just forty-two years of age.

General McIntosh quickly recovered from his wound and lived another three decades.

All this brings to mind the most famous duel in American history between Aaron Burr and Alexander Hamilton.

After Hamilton was fatally wounded in that exchange, it has been reported that he observed before passing: "*I have lived like a man, but I die like a fool.*"

CHAPTER THIRTEEN

Lyman Hall

L yman Hall was born in Connecticut sometime between 1721 and 1724. Like a number of the eventual Founding Fathers, he was born into some degree of wealth and when of age he attended and graduated from Yale College around 1747.

Although an ordained minister, he decided that his chosen profession would be in the practice of medicine. During those early years, he married Abigail Burr, who tragically passed but a year later. After some time, Hall married again, this time to Mary Osborne. She and Hall were soon blessed with the birth of a son.

In 1758 Hall joined about forty other New England families in relocating to the town of Sunbury in the St. John's Parish of Georgia. Once established in that town and area, Hall's medical practice began to thrive.

But as it grew, so did his resentment against the Crown, a resentment that firmly took hold within him after the Stamp Act of 1765. As detailed, this act of oppression galvanized a majority of the Founding Fathers into action against the "mother country." The tax also proved to be the last straw the Crown laid upon the already trembling backs of the colonists.

While many Americans mistakenly blame King George III for instituting the Stamp Act, it was in fact the prime minister of Great Britain, George Grenville.

England was having its own monetary problems, and Grenville thought a solution to mitigate that strain on the economy was to impose punishing taxes upon the American colonies, with the first being the Sugar Act of 1764. Next came the more onerous Stamp Act of 1765, which infuriated the majority of the **Founding Fathers** and solidified their determination to separate from Great Britain. **Lyman Hall** was one Patriot so inspired to speak out.

Quite ironically, he and those other forty New England families—who could not stand the dictates of England—had relocated into a colony in which a majority of the inhabitants were still extremely loyal to the Crown.

Whoops.

While the colony may have been pro-British, the town of Sunbury was not.

Just the opposite. Because the entire town *was populated* by transplanted families from New England—families who had already deeply resented the Crown *before* moving to Georgia. Sunbury and its surrounding parish had become a hotbed of growing insurrection against Great Britain.

That reality put **Lyman Hall** into a bit of a precarious situation. The revolutionary rhetoric being spoken by the medical doctor from New England, looking to recruit more and more of the people to his Patriotic cause, was also working to greatly antagonize the massive number of Loyalists around him.

As Hall was dealing with that worrisome reality, he was also becoming increasingly frustrated by the failure of the conventions he attended in Savannah in both 1774 and 1775 to agree to send any delegates to the Continental Congress.

Not only was Hall greatly upset by this inaction but so were the vast majority of people in St. John's Parish. They were so frustrated that they made it quite clear they were prepared to *secede* from the colony if necessary. Toward that end, the parish held its own convention in March of 1775 and named **Lyman Hall** as its personal delegate to the Continental Congress.

Impressed by this move of Revolutionary independence, the membership of the Continental Congress decided to accept Hall as a "nonvoting" member. Fortunately, come July of 1775, Georgia saw the writing on the wall and decided to not only officially sanction Hall as a delegate, but also to appoint two others in the process.

Soon after, the war was in full bloom, and **Lyman Hall**—like a number of Founding Fathers—paid a high price for daring to sign the **Declaration of Independence**. When Savannah fell to the British in 1778, his home was singled out for destruction, his possessions burned, and his property confiscated.

He and his family avoided capture and were able to escape to the North. Upon his return to Georgia, he resumed his medical practice while attempting to rebuild his life.

Not only was Hall successful in that endeavor, but in 1783 he was elected to the state legislature and later he was elected governor.

Lyman Hall passed in 1790 at sixty-six years of age.

CHAPTER FOURTEEN

George Walton

George Walton is the last of the three signers from Georgia. He is also one of the few **Founding Fathers** whose exact birthdate could never be established. That noted, he was born sometime in the **1740s** in Frederick County, Virginia.

Unlike many of the Founding Fathers, not only was he born into a very poor family, but he found himself sadly orphaned at a very early age. He was taken in by an uncle who was not only also struggling financially, but who also felt that education for a young lad like Walton was a complete waste of time and immediately apprenticed him as his carpenter's assistant seven days a week for hour upon hour.

Knowing his stern uncle did not want him to read, write, or learn, young Walton would save the small pieces of waste wood from his nonstop carpentry work and, when his uncle would go to sleep, would light that scrapwood on fire while in hiding to provide a meager amount of light to study on his own.

When he was a bit older and felt he was able, the by-then self-educated Walton left his uncle's care in **1769** and moved to the colony of Georgia where he commenced the study of law. By 1774, Walton had been quite impressively admitted to the bar. Even more impressively for him, he met, fell in love with, and married a young woman by the name of Dorothy Camber.

Around that same time, Walton had become acquainted with a few of the more outspoken Patriots in the area, not the least among them was **Lyman Hall**.

Because of his impoverished childhood, coupled with the sometimes-abusive treatment by his uncle, Walton had adopted an independent streak long before relocating to Georgia. As such, it did not take much discussion from Hall or the others Patriots to convince him that the Crown was slowly choking the life out of the colonies.

By 1776, Walton had become one of the more vocal and respected Revolutionaries in Georgia. He was deeply disturbed that the colony was full of Loyalists and was never shy about making his disgust over that reality known far and wide. For those reasons and others, in that same year he was elected to the Second Continental Congress, where in addition to voting for independence and then signing the Declaration, he served on the committees for the national finance, the western lands, and Indian affairs.

But for Walton, even those acts of defiance were not enough. He was still itching for a fight and felt the best way to scratch that itch was by becoming a member of the Georgia Militia.

Once again, watch out what you wish for.

In 1778, Walton was commissioned a colonel in the First Regiment of that militia, the 1st Georgia.

In December of that year, then Colonel Walton was wounded in the battle to try and save Savannah from a British invasion. After being shot in the leg and falling from his horse, he was immediately taken prisoner by the redcoats.

The British officers soon realized that Walton was one of the "traitorous signers" and used his elevated status to demand that a redcoat brigadier general be freed in exchange for Walton.

After spending approximately nine months in a horrendous British prisoner of war camp, he was finally exchanged for a redcoat officer.

Nine months of Crown mistreatment did nothing to quell the fire of independence burning within Walton. Not long after his release, he made his way back home, where he became chief justice of the state superior court, a US senator, and the governor of Georgia.

George Walton passed in February **1804** in his early to midsixties.

Chapter Fifteen

William Hooper

It's never a good thing to be thought of as a "Political Weathervane turning in the winds of self-interest,"[22] and **William Hooper** had that epithet hung around his neck by some of his fellow colonists.

Should you forget what a "political weathervane" looks like, simply google the face of almost anyone presently serving in the Congress of the United States of today. That will refresh your memory.

William Hooper was born in Boston on **June 17, 1742**. His father was a minister from Scotland as well as a graduate of the University of Edinburgh. Unfortunately for young Hooper, his father was also considered by many to be a Loyalist to the Crown, a bias that did not go over well with the Revolutionary population of Boston.

Was Hooper influenced by his father's beliefs? It would be hard to imagine that he was not. This trait evidenced itself years later when both those winds of war and personal self-interest began blowing against his face.

While his father wanted him to follow in his footsteps and become a minister, Hooper at least showed enough backbone to defy his father on that request. He enrolled in Harvard College and upon graduation proceeded to study law under **James Otis**, the somewhat famous Boston attorney who in 1761 uttered the phrase *"Taxation without representation is tyranny."*

In about 1764, young Hooper decided he had had enough of Boston and relocated to Wilmington, North Carolina, to set up his legal practice. Some have speculated that he fled Boston because his Loyalist tendencies were already coming to the attention of some of the tough guys in town strongly opposed to the Crown. Others guessed that because **James Otis** had become a political influence upon him, Hooper was upsetting his Loyalist family and decided to leave for that reason. Whatever the reason, he did move to North Carolina to establish a new life, which soon included Anne Clark as his wife.

Hooper for sure had political aspirations, and by 1770 he had been appointed as the deputy attorney general of North Carolina. By then, his reputation for making "self-serving" decisions was already growing among some of his fellow citizens within the colony.

Never was that more evident than during that same year when an insurrection movement began by a group of colonists who called themselves the "Regulators." The Regulators had been born in desperation as a last-ditch attempt to fight back against the crippling and cruel policies of the then-royal governor by the name of Tryon. In many Patriotic ways, the men who made up the Regulators were the North Carolina version of the **Sons of Liberty**.

The fact is, Governor Tryon was an especially cruel tyrant who enjoyed inflicting pain and even death upon those calling themselves the Regulators.

Unfortunately for the Regulators and their wives and children, **William Hooper** decided to align himself with the despicable Tryon against them. He did so, and with Hooper's advice and consent, Tryon was able to crush the growing rebellion against him.

The Patriots of North Carolina immediately branded Hooper a "royalist" and a "traitor."

But, somehow in the face of that reputation-destroying narrative, Hooper was somehow able to flip the script and within two years magically align himself with the Patriots in the colony fighting the growing oppression of the Crown.

Had Hooper been alive today, he might have been teaching the "Master Class" to Congress on how best and when to morph into a slimy chameleon to screw over their constituents while enriching themselves in the process.

Whether his political and loyalty flip-flop was genuine or gutless, only the late Mr. Hooper will ever really know. That said, the flip was a success, garnering all nines and tens from the North Carolina judges.

In 1774, he was elected to the First Continental Congress and reelected in 1776. On August 2 of that year, he signed the **Declaration of Independence**.

Again, was this newly proclaimed blast of Patriotism the real thing, or was he merely covering all bets?

By 1777, Hooper had resigned his seat in Congress to return to his estate on the outskirts Wilmington, North Carolina. After the British invaded the colony in 1780, he sent his family into the city to keep them safe.

While Hooper was conveniently away on business in January of 1781, Wilmington fell to the British Army, and Hooper was separated from his family for almost a year.

When the redcoats finally did evacuate the city, Hooper returned to luckily find his family safe, but his estate had been destroyed as punishment for his being one of the signers of the **Declaration of Independence**.

After the war, he tried to adopt an even more Patriotic political philosophy, but by that time many of his fellow North Carolinians were not sure what to believe about him, and he quickly lost favor among much of the population.

With the tide of public opinion turning against him, **William Hooper** passed in 1790 at forty-eight years of age.

CHAPTER SIXTEEN

Joseph Hewes

𝕴magine being the personal advocate for 𝕵𝖔𝖍𝖓 𝕻𝖆𝖚𝖑 𝕵𝖔𝖓𝖊𝖘—only the most highly decorated and honored Naval war hero of the American Revolution—and getting shot down by…𝕵𝖔𝖍𝖓 𝕬𝖉𝖆𝖒𝖘. Ouch.

Such was the unpleasant reality faced by 𝕵𝖔𝖘𝖊𝖕𝖍 𝕳𝖊𝖜𝖊𝖘.

The parents of Hewes were both members of what was known then as the "Society of Friends," or later better known as the Quakers. After their marriage, they left Connecticut and moved just outside Princeton, New Jersey. It was there that 𝕵𝖔𝖘𝖊𝖕𝖍 𝕳𝖊𝖜𝖊𝖘 was born in 1730.

After growing to young adulthood, he secured his education at Princeton and then moved to Philadelphia to apprentice as a merchant. After satisfactorily learning the business, Hewes decided to strike out on his own and, at approximately thirty years of age, moved to a small seaport town by the name of Edenton in North Carolina.

After Hewes established himself in the town, some reports have him meeting and falling in love with a young woman by the name of Isabella Johnson. Tragically, those same sources indicate that it appears she passed away just days before she and Hewes were to be married.

Reportedly beyond devastated by the loss, Hewes decided to deal with his heartache by pouring all his energy, emotions, and incredible work ethic into first, business, and then a few years later, the politics of his colony.

And pour them in, he did. Already highly respected by his community, Hewes was quickly elected to the North Carolina provincial assembly in 1766, the committee of Correspondence in 1773, and the Continental Congress in 1774.

Now, it is at that time that things really got interesting for Joseph Hewes. After being elected to the Continental Congress, he was appointed to head the Naval Committee.

In that capacity, Hewes truly was the very first secretary of the navy for the United States. Because of his decades-long experience as a maritime merchant, Hewes not only took the position very seriously, but he also felt because of his experience, he had identified the greatest sailor he had ever known. That man was John Paul Jones.

Now, pardon my language, but Jones truly was the badass of all badasses when it came to being a tough-as-nails sailor and commander.

Hewes also felt those winds of war blowing across the coast of North Carolina and knew you didn't send weak angels into battles against inhuman monsters.

To offer a more modern example of this, a few decades ago, the late, truly great comedian Richard Pryor spoke to this fact in a joking manner before a sold-out audience. When speaking of the attack on Pearl Harbor by the Japanese in 1941, Pryor related that before that attack in the mid- to late-1930s, a number of Japanese students and future Japanese military officers had gone to school at UCLA and USC in California and noted that the weak, little American men on those campuses could barely carry their own book bags, let alone win a fight. Based on that research, Pryor joked, the Japanese decided to attack.

But, as Pryor observed, the Japanese had sorely miscalculated. For as soon as the war began, the United States unchained the massive, snarling, barking behemoths at the University of Alabama and the University of Georgia, and it was soon lights-out for the Japanese.

In many real ways, Hewes knew that **John Paul Jones** was one of those "snarling, barking behemoths" that could be let off his chain when needed and would do what was necessary to win the war.

How much of a badass was Jones?

To begin with, his real name wasn't even Jones. It was John Paul. He added "Jones" later after he personally killed the leader of a mutiny on his ship.

John Paul was born in Scotland on **July 6, 1747**. By thirteen years of age, John Paul started his life on the seas and in many ways never looked back. By his early twenties, John Paul had moved up the ranks to command his own ships. It was while he was commanding a ship known as the *Betsy* that his life—and the future of Revolutionary America—changed forever.

One of the men on that ship decided to lead a mutiny against John Paul and the other officers. In self-defense, John Paul ran the man through with his sword.

As the man he killed had influential family members back in Scotland, John Paul decided he did not want to put his life in the hands of an admiralty court.

That decided, he fled to Fredericksburg, Virginia, where his older brother, William, had already made a life for himself.

Sometime after that, he felt it might be wise to add the "Jones" to his name to give himself one more layer of cover.

In 1775, John Paul Jones decided he wanted to fight on the side of his new home country and headed to Philadelphia to sign up with the Continental Navy. By 1776, he was given command of his own vessel, and while on his first cruise aboard the *Providence*, he proceeded to Nova Scotia, where he not only destroyed the British fisheries he encountered but also captured sixteen British ships in the process.

Through 1777 and 1778, John Paul Jones operated in British home waters, where he continually bested their fleet while also capturing more of their ships.

On September 23, 1779, Jones fought in his most famous battle. For it was then, while commanding the *Bonhomme Richard* that he engaged with the powerful, forty-four-gun Royal Navy Frigate *Serapis*. It was one of the bloodiest and most vicious battles in naval history to that point.

Seeing the *Bonhomme Richard* aflame and sinking, the British commander sent word to Jones to surrender. With his by-then usual flamboyant flair, Jones replied: "*Sir, I have not yet begun to fight.*"

True to his word, after almost three more hours of constant bombardment and fighting, it was the British commander who surrendered his ship to Jones.

To be sure, John Paul Jones was every bit the swashbuckler.

He was a prolific writer, spoke several languages, dressed impeccably, believed deeply in honor, was a legendary ladies' man, and could be an engaging personality when the occasion called.

But above all, he could flip a switch and instantly morph into the harshest of military leaders when needed.

It was this side of him that made him a cultlike figure in Great Britain, where the earliest versions of dime novels portrayed him as a ruthless pirate no better than Blackbeard.

While some in the Continental Navy may have been put off by his larger-than-life personality and accomplishments, one woman was not. The most powerful woman in the world at that time: *Catherine the Great* of Russia. She came to deeply admire the personality and skill of Jones—and maybe a bit more, according to the speculation of the day—and appointed him a rear admiral of her navy in 1778.

All of that is to say that **Joseph Hewes** was truly on to something when he became a friend and advocate to **John Paul Jones**.

As some snippets of history of the time tell us, as the head of the Naval Committee Hewes had nominated Jones for one of America's first naval captaincies based on Jones's vast experience and skill.

Unfortunately for Hewes, **John Adams** of Boston—also on the committee—decided to big-foot Hewes and object to the nomination of Jones.

In this particular case, I will say my fellow Bostonian Adams flipped his powdered wig and put hubris before country.

Adams felt that because the New Englanders on the Continental Congress had already agreed to let the Virginian **George Washington** become commander in chief of the Continental Army, all naval captaincies should go to New Englanders.

While losing that rhetorical battle to Adams, **Joseph Hewes** was also losing his physical battle with life. Soon after being reelected to the Continental Congress in 1779, he passed at forty-nine years of age.

CHAPTER SEVENTEEN

John Penn

nlike his eventual fellow cosigner of the Declaration, Button Gwinnet, John Penn had no intention of being shot in a duel to which he would one day be challenged.

Penn was born in the county of Caroline, Virginia, on May 17, 1741. Penn's father also saw any formal education as a complete waste of time for his son and therefore only afforded him the bare minimum.

That said, young Penn had a deeply curious mind and was desperate to learn. Fortunately for him, he was related to a then very famous Virginian by the name of Edmund Pendleton, a man who himself would become a member of the House of Burgesses and be elected to the Continental Congress.

At the time, Pendleton had an extensive library and gave young Penn free use of it and the hundreds of books it contained. Inspired by the knowledge before him, Penn decided to pursue his own legal study in the hopes of becoming an attorney. Penn succeeded in that single-minded self-education pursuit and was admitted to the Virginia bar at twenty-one years of age.

After practicing law for several years in Virginia, he uprooted himself, his new wife, Susannah Lyne, and at least one child, and moved down to Granville County, North Carolina, in 1774.

Once settled into North Carolina, Penn almost immediately began to take up the Patriot cause and speak out against the oppression of the Crown. Soon, the heretofore quiet and unassuming gentleman was elected to the Continental Congress in 1775. Aside from voting for American independence on July 2, 1776, and then signing the Declaration of Independence, Penn also had the honor of being one of the few Founding Fathers to also sign the Articles of Confederation.

As mentioned, by nature Penn was quiet and nonconfrontational. All the more reason it was remarkable the dire situation he soon found himself facing.

While Penn could get along with just about anyone, there was one member of the Continental Congress who he really could not stomach: Henry Laurens, who just happened to be the president of that body at the time.

It is said that Penn and Laurens disagreed regularly, with things getting heated but never quite boiling over. That all changed when on one day, their disagreement over policy and the ensuing argument became so intense that Laurens challenged Penn to a duel, and for whatever reason, Penn heard himself agreeing to the duel.

No matter whatever pride, stupidity, or temporary insanity caused him to agree to such a deadly entanglement, Penn decided he needed to stop the momentum in its tracks before it was literally too late.

As it turned out, both men were staying in the same boarding house in Philadelphia at the time. In what might seem quite odd to anyone looking at the two soon to be combatants from afar, both men decided to have breakfast together the morning of their scheduled duel.

But what might seem odd to some was really a sign that the tension between both men had already cooled. The only problem now was that neither man knew how to back out of the duel without losing "honor."

After breakfast, both men walked in silence toward the vacant lot they had selected to fight it out. As they were approaching the lot, there was a large ditch in the road. Penn easily stepped across it and then turned to offer a helping hand to the much older Laurens.

After helping him across, Penn shook his head, looked Laurens in the eye, and said something along the lines of: "This is completely foolish. Neither of us has the will for it and we should call it off."

The older Laurens nodded his head, smiled, and instantly agreed.

Just like that, the duel was called off.

Penn lived to see another year but, sadly, not a great many more.

Once back home, Penn was appointed to the North Carolina Board of War in 1780, which was dissolved one year later because others in the state viewed it as a threat to their power.

In 1781, Penn was next offered a position on the Governor's Council. However, because he felt his health waning at the time, he declined the offer. Three years later, he did agree to become the state tax receiver for a period, but the position proved so unpopular with his fellow citizens that he soon resigned and spent the time he had remaining on Earth involved with his beloved practice of law.

John Penn passed in 1788 at forty-seven years of age.

Chapter Eighteen

Edward Rutledge

What truly significant accomplishment were you able to mark by the time you reached twenty-six years of age?

Edward Rutledge was able to check the box for being the youngest signer of the **Declaration of Independence**.

It's easy to imagine that such an unrivaled achievement came in handy over the years as he was listening to usual pompous family members or friends drone on about how much money they had, how big the fish was they just caught, or how luxurious was the horse and buggy they just purchased.

"Gee," Rutledge could have smirked. "Me being the youngest signer of the document that created our Republic pales in comparison to that twenty-inch trout. Good for you."

Moving on to his history, **Edward Rutledge** was born in Charleston, South Carolina, in November **1749**. He was the youngest of seven children born to a very successful doctor and his very wealthy wife.

When the father of Rutledge passed, his mother was but twenty-seven years of age. Fortunately, while sadly a widow, she did not have to worry about money. And neither did young

Rutledge. His mother saw to it that he was not only educated in the classics but would also receive his higher education back in Great Britain.

And what an education it turned out to be.

Rutledge became a student at the "Inner Temple" of London. Just what was—or is—the Inner Temple? As was reported over 175 years ago:

> A number of Inns of Court, or sort of colleges for teaching the law were established in London at various times. The Temple (of which there were three societies, the Inner, the Middle, and the Outer) was originally founded and the Temple Church, built by The Knights Templar, in the reign of Henry II, 1185.

Now, if you go to the website for the Inner Temple of today, its history page relates:

> In the middle of the 12th century, the Military Order of the Knights Templar built a fine round church by the Thames, which became known as the Temple Church. Two centuries later, after the abolition of the Order in 1312, lawyers came to occupy the Temple site and buildings. They formed themselves into two societies, the Inner Temple and Middle Temple.[23]

The entries are almost identical. What is *not* the same is the ideological makeup of the Inner Temple from when

Rutledge attended to today. When he was there in approximately 1769, its teachings were conservative, pragmatic, and faith-based.

Today, it seemingly lurches more and more into the world of the woke as it promotes its social-justice warrior credentials while weakening its once laudable standards.

But hey, why should the Inner Temple be different from every other liberal to Far Left University in the country and world? It's no longer the students who matter or their futures but indoctrination, tenure, and most of all...*money*.

Going back to the youngest signer of the **Declaration of Independence**, Rutledge returned to South Carolina toward the end of 1772 and began his legal practice in 1773.

While in London and at the Inner Temple, he often heard the British elite and political class refer to the American colonists as second-class citizens and a people to be looked down upon and taken advantage of when necessary.

As he was on the ship back home from Great Britain, he was already cementing his Patriotic roots based on those snobbish beliefs and insults coupled with the punitive policy decisions already implemented by the Crown against the colonies. By the time he set foot back in Charleston, he was ready to engage in the fight.

Almost immediately upon his return, Rutledge loudly signaled his loyalty to the Patriotic cause and budding Revolution by using his considerable legal skills to obtain the release of a local newspaper publisher who had been imprisoned by the Crown for printing an article critical of the Loyalist members of the colonial legislature.

This scenario sounds more and more familiar to us in 2022 with regard to anyone who dares to question the dictates of the totalitarian left.

Going back to Rutledge, in many ways, 1774 proved to be the most momentous year of his life. At twenty-four years of age, he married Henrietta Middleton, a member of a very wealthy and incredibly prominent and powerful family.

How prominent and powerful? Well, both her father and her brother were members of the Continental Congress and her brother—like her new husband—would go on to sign the **Declaration of Independence**.

No pressure or intimidation factor there at all for young Rutledge!

Soon after his marriage however, Rutledge himself was elected to the Continental Congress. Suddenly, he had a bit more of an equal footing with the in-laws.

Not that he really needed it. For as soon as he was elected, he hit the ground running and his passion and considerable talents became evident to all, most especially **Richard Henry Lee** and **John Adams**.

By late 1776—after voting for and then signing the **Declaration of Independence**—Rutledge took a leave from the Continental Congress to go back home to Charleston to literally fight for his friends, neighbors, and family.

He was appointed to an artillery battalion in the defense of his colony and fought in a number of critical battles against the British while rising to the rank of captain.

Unfortunately, when Charleston fell to the redcoats in 1780, Rutledge, along with his brother-in-law **Arthur Middleton** and **Thomas Heyward Jr.**—both also signers of the

Declaration—were taken prisoners by the British, sent to a prisoner-of-war camp in Florida for a year, and treated quite inhumanely at times. The abuse affected the health of all three men in their later years.

After his release in July of 1781, Rutledge endeavored to return to his normal and political life. In 1782, he was elected to the state legislature, where he served on almost twenty different committees.

During those years, Rutledge—along with a number of other Patriots in South Carolina—had been targeted and even assaulted by Loyalists in the state, working in concert with the Crown to crush the Revolution.

Because of that treatment, coupled with his year in the prisoner-of-war camp enduring the most horrendous of conditions, Rutledge formed an angry and hardened position against the Loyalists of his colony. He wanted them punished.

One way he sought to do so was by introducing a bill that would allow for the confiscation of property belonging to Loyalists. This bill proved quite popular among a number of his fellow citizens.

It was so popular that Rutledge was elected governor of South Carolina in 1798. Tragically, the abuse he had suffered earlier at the hands of his British captors began to catch up with him, and his health quickly deteriorated.

"Young" **Edward Rutledge** never finished his first term as governor and passed in 1800 at just fifty years of age.

CHAPTER NINETEEN

Thomas Heyward Jr.

Again, while many on the Left and far left want to diminish, invalidate, or outright ban our Independence Day, fortunately tens of millions of Americans not only still cherish it but also proudly celebrate it on its annual arrival.

That said, none of them can hold a candle to **Thomas Heyward Jr.** when it comes to passionate, fun, and spread-like-wildfire ways to commemorate the most important date in the history of our nation.

At the end of June 1781, Heyward had been a prisoner of the British for almost a year. As just mentioned, he, along with fellow signers **Edward Rutledge** and **Arthur Middleton,** had suffered tremendous abuse at the hands of their captors. That said, the spirit of none of them was broken. Least of all, Heyward.

Not only was he courageous to the extreme, but he was also quite clever and creative. As such, and just before his release and in honor of the upcoming Independence Day, he decided to patriotically change the words of the British National Anthem—"God Save the King"—into **"God Save the Thirteen States."**

Not only was it an "in your face" to his brutal jailers, but it proved to be immensely popular as it spread from one end of the colonies to the other.

𝔗homas 𝔥eyward 𝔍r. was born into one of the wealthiest families in St. Luke's Parish, South Carolina, in 1746. As a child and young adult, he wanted for nothing.

He was enrolled in the best school in the region and proved to be an exceptional student. So good, in fact, that he read the works of ancient Roman historians and poets in the original Latin.

With a growing interest in the law, young Heyward was sent by his father to London to be educated at one of the Inns of Court at the Temple and former stomping grounds of the Knights Templar.

While there, he also came to hear the British elites refer to the American colonists in the most condescending and insulting of manners. He became so incensed by such talk that he was determined to travel back home to assist in breaking the bondage of such transatlantic oppression.

Before leaving for home, Heyward took it upon himself to travel about the Continent. Instead of being impressed by the famous capitals and "civilized" existence, he was deeply disturbed to note that the elites of those nations were also abusing the millions of "unwashed masses" under their care.

Once finally back in South Carolina, he dove right into both his legal career and his political aspirations. In 1772, Heyward was elected to the colonial legislature.

Approximately one year later, he married Elizabeth Matthews. Not only was she quite accomplished in her own right, but as it turned out, her brother also served in the Continental Congress and became the governor of South

Carolina. That brother was John Mathews, who years later would marry the sister of signer **Edward Rutledge**.

Small—*colonial*—world indeed.

In 1776, Heyward was elected to the Second Continental Congress and had the distinction of being one of the few signers of both the **Declaration of Independence** and the **Articles of Confederation**.

After leaving the Continental Congress in 1778, Heyward returned home to accept an appointment as a circuit judge.

Now, to go back and connect the dots to the beginning of this small bio on Heyward, in 1779 he joined the state militia as a captain of an artillery battalion. During the Battle of Port Royal Island, he was wounded. Upon recovery, he was right back in the war. While commanding a militia force during the siege of Charleston in 1780, he, along with two fellow South Carolina signers **Edward Rutledge** and **Arthur Middleton**, was taken prisoner by the British.

While prisoner—and because he had an indelible red target on his back as one of the "traitorous" signers of the Declaration—the British plundered and desecrated his home estate.

Once freed, Heyward returned home to rebuild his life. He did so by resuming his judgeship, serving in the state legislature, and even helping to found the Agricultural Society of South Carolina.

Thomas Heyward Jr. passed in 1809 at sixty-two years of age.

CHAPTER TWENTY

Thomas Lynch Jr.

Next, we come to another Thomas Jr. This one being a "Lynch."

𝕿homas 𝕷ynch 𝕵r. has two important historical notes attached to his name—the first being that at just twenty-seven years of age, he was the second youngest to sign the Declaration after his fellow South Carolinian 𝕰dward 𝕽utledge.

The next historical note was quite tragic. He lost his life at a younger age than any other of the other 55 𝕾igners. He died at age thirty when he and all aboard a ship headed to the south of France were lost at sea.

𝕿homas 𝕷ynch 𝕵r. was born into wealth on 𝕬ugust 5, 1749, in Prince George's Parish, South Carolina. At just thirteen years of age, he was sent to England to attain his higher education, first attending Eton and then the University of Cambridge.

Upon his return to South Carolina in 1772, he established his law practice and then soon married Elizabeth Shubrick.

Lynch's wealthy and prominent father was strongly opposed to the Crown's oppressive tactics, and his beliefs and emotions rubbed off on his only son. For that reason and others, Lynch enlisted in the First South Carolina Regiment, where he was made a captain.

Unfortunately, while on a recruiting trip to North Carolina, Captain Lynch may have contracted malaria. Whatever the sickness was, he never fully recovered and became a partial invalid. That said, Lynch refused to let that handicap interfere with his Patriotic zeal. In March 1776, Lynch was elected as a member of the Continental Congress, a body his esteemed father had served in until he was afflicted by a stroke.

Upon his selection, **Thomas Lynch Jr**. made the approximately 600-mile journey to not only join his very sick father in Philadelphia but also to participate in his first Continental Congress.

As young Lynch was already an invalid because of his malaria, he arrived in Philadelphia quite weak. More troubling to him, he found his beloved father in even worse shape.

With his father too ill to attend the signing of the **Declaration of Independence**, the younger Lynch managed to make his way over and add his own signature to what would soon amount to **The 56**.

That glorious deed accomplished, he wanted to get his father home as rapidly as possible so he might get better medical care. Sadly, while en route, his father suffered a second, fatal stroke.

Heartbroken and chronically ill himself, Lynch retired from all politics and activities and returned to the comfort of his family estate.

As his own health continued to wane, Lynch was convinced that the climate in the south of France might bring about an improvement. Believing that to be true, he and his dear wife, Elizabeth, boarded a ship for France in 1779. He, his wife, and all aboard were soon lost.

Again, 𝔗homas 𝔏ynch 𝔍r.—the second-youngest signer— was just thirty years of age.

CHAPTER TWENTY-ONE

Arthur Middleton

With regard to the Revolutionary life of young 𝕰𝖉𝖜𝖆𝖗𝖉 𝕽𝖚𝖙𝖑𝖊𝖉𝖌𝖊, we learned that he did carry a bit of a grudge when it came to the Loyalists in South Carolina and wanted their property confiscated as retribution for their siding with the Crown against the colonies.

As it turned out, Rutledge was a softie compared to his brother-in-law. 𝕬𝖗𝖙𝖍𝖚𝖗 𝕸𝖎𝖉𝖉𝖑𝖊𝖙𝖔𝖓 not only wanted to confiscate the property of those he viewed as despicable traitors to the cause of independence, but he also wanted them "tarred and feathered."

A year of abuse, starvation, and torture in a Crown prisoner-of-war camp will do that to a man.

Middleton was born at "Middleton Place" just outside Charleston, South Carolina, around 1742. The very fact that he was given birth on the grounds of a massive estate named after his family confirms his station in life at that time.

As mentioned in the chapter of Rutledge, Middleton's father was not only a member of the Continental Congress but also one of the wealthiest men in all of the colonies.

When he was of age, his father sent Arthur to England for the remainder of his education. Middleton was serious, studious, and graduated with honors from the University of Cambridge at about twenty-one years of age.

As he had relatives still living in Great Britain, he decided to stay a while to get to know them better. "A while" stretched into months, as he also decided that if he was ever going to travel about the Continent, that was the time to do so.

His favorite stop on his tour of enlightenment may have been the city of Rome. He not only fell in love with the people and the culture, but he also became fairly proficient as a painter as well.

All good things do come to an end, and the time soon came for Arthur to head back to South Carolina, which he did about 1763 after almost a decade in Europe.

Approximately one year later, he married a young woman by the name of Mary Izard. Just about that same time, he was also elected to the South Carolina legislature.

With each day that he was back in South Carolina the fire in Middleton burned hotter for the colonies to gain independence from the Crown. The young man not only wore his emotions on his sleeve, but he would back down from no man—Loyalist or redcoat—to make his opinion known.

How dedicated was Middleton to the cause? While serving as a member of the provisional assemblies, he helped to organize a night raid on public arms stores before the royal governor could have them seized, raised funds for the armed resistance to the British, and helped to draft plans to defend the harbor of Charleston.

In 1776, he was elected to replace his ailing father in the Continental Congress. After taking the time to sign the

Declaration of Independence, young Middleton headed back to South Carolina to continue the military defense of his colony.

With that singular goal in mind, he joined the South Carolina Militia in 1780. When Charleston fell to the British redcoats, Middleton, like Rutledge and Heyward Jr., was taken prisoner and treated abysmally.

Spoiler alert…while Middleton was held captive, he not only lost his entire fortune, but the British Army also plundered and destroyed his estate as added punishment for signing the Declaration.

Once released, he spent the majority of his time trying to reestablish his home and property. When not working on that, he still managed to serve in the state legislature while being one of the original trustees of the College of Charleston.

Like Rutledge and Heyward Jr., the punishment he absorbed while a prisoner of war took a tremendous toll on his body.

Arthur Middleton passed away in 1787 at just forty-four years of age.

CHAPTER TWENTY-TWO

Samuel Chase

Most people would not like to be referred to as "*a busy, reckless incendiary, a ringleader of mobs, a foul-mouthed and inflaming son of discord and faction, and a common disturber of the public tranquility.*"[24]

But, as those charges and insults were hurled at 𝕾amuel 𝕮hase by fellow Marylanders loyal to the British Crown, Chase wore them proudly like a badge of honor.

If anything, he didn't believe they were nearly accurate enough, as he knew he was being *much more* disrespectful to the Crown than that and wanted the proper hate-filled credit from the Loyalist scum.

Chase was born on 𝖆pril 17, 1741, in Somerset County, Maryland. Sadly, his mother passed while giving birth to him, and he was raised by his minister father. His father strongly believed his son should have as much of a classical education as possible. But because of the limited financial resources of the family, Chase was mostly homeschooled by his highly educated father and proved to be an exceptional student desperate for knowledge.

By his late teens, Chase had decided he wanted to enter the profession of law and apprenticed with a prestigious practice in Annapolis. By the age of twenty-two he was admitted to the bar.

In and around that same time, he met and married a young woman by the name of Anne Baldwin.

But as his career was taking off, so was his growing resentment of the Crown. **Samuel Chase** had supreme confidence that his position against the oppressive tactics of the Crown and in favor of American independence was the correct one, and he was more than happy to state it. No matter if the person wanted to hear it or not.

Even at that, for Chase rhetorical resistance was not enough. If he was truly going to walk the walk, then he felt he had to step up his game against the Crown. And step it up he did.

As mentioned, all "revolutionary" roads in America eventually intersected the punitive Stamp Act of 1765 rolled out by the Crown as a way to further soak the colonial taxpayers. It was an act that definitely fired up Chase and a number of his friends, one of whom was **William Paca**, who would also go on to sign the **Declaration of Independence**.

If imitation is the sincerest form of flattery, then **Samuel Adams** and some of the toughs walking the streets of Boston in those days had to be quite happy with the conduct of Chase and his friends.

As was reported over 175 years ago regarding Chase and his anti-Crown actions:

> He was one of a band of young Patriots, who,
> in imitation of those of Massachusetts, styled

themselves "**Sons of Liberty.**" They opposed the operation of the Stamp Act in every form, and even went so far as to assault the Stamp offices, and destroy the Stamps.[25]

More than that, it has also been reported that in that same late time period of 1765, Chase and his friends also made and then burned an effigy of the local stamp distributor, with Chase himself setting it aflame. Hard to imagine why the Marylanders loyal to the oppressive Crown would take exception to Chase and start calling him names!

Aside from the rhetorical and the civil disobedience acts of protest, Chase also knew that the political was even more important if the colonies were to secure their freedom. With that in mind, in 1774 and 1775, Chase served in the Maryland Committee of Correspondence, the Committee of Safety, and the Provincial convention.

Of those, the Committee of Correspondence was the most vital. Why? As eminent historian B.J. Lossing reported over 175 years ago:

> These Committees of Correspondence con-
> stituted a powerful agent in the great work
> of the Revolution. Their conception was si-
> multaneous in Massachusetts and Virginia
> (Samuel Adams and Richard Henry Lee), and
> both States claim the honor of priority. At
> first these Committees were confined to the
> larger cities, but very speedily every village
> and hamlet had its auxiliary Committees, and
> the high moral tone evinced by the Chiefs, ran

through all the gradations, from the polished committees appointed by Colonial Assemblies to the rustic, yet not the least Patriotic ones of the interior towns; and through these made an impression upon the whole American people. Thus the Patriotic heart of America, at this crisis, beat as with one pulsation, and the public mind was fully prepared to act with promptness and decision when circumstances should call for action.

This "call for action" eventually would be shouted out all across the colonies.

Samuel Chase not only heard that call but also knew his passion had to find a higher level of activity and achievement. He found those plateaus in 1774 when he was also elected to the First Continental Congress. His election to that body was critical as it was mostly his voice of passion that convinced the Maryland delegation to vote for independence on July 2, 1776.

After the Revolutionary War, he served Maryland first as the chief justice of the Criminal Court of Baltimore and from 1791 as the chief justice of the Maryland Superior Court.

In 1796, President George Washington appointed Chase as an associate justice of the United States Supreme Court, an office he held until his passing fifteen years later.

But because this is Samuel Chase we are talking about, his tenure on the Court was not without controversy. Even as a justice on the Supreme Court, Chase regularly let his personal political opinions be known. Opinions, he stressed, that would never interfere with his impartiality on the Court.

Naturally, others disagreed, most especially those with long memories who had issues with Chase over the decades. They sought to impeach him for his personal views and were successful in getting the House of Representatives to vote for that outcome. Fortunately for Chase, the Senate found him not guilty of the charges, and he was able to retain his position on the highest court of the land.

Chase's controversial impeachment helped to set the precedent that judges should not be removed from office for personal political beliefs.

𝔖amuel 𝔆hase passed away in Baltimore in 1811 at seventy years of age.

CHAPTER TWENTY-THREE

William Paca

At least to the British Crown and its Loyalists in Maryland, 𝔚𝔦𝔩𝔩𝔦𝔞𝔪 𝔓𝔞𝔠𝔞 was a pea from the same pod of insurrection that had spit out 𝔖𝔞𝔪𝔲𝔢𝔩 𝔆𝔥𝔞𝔰𝔢.

In another word, "trouble."

Paca was born at Wye Hall—his paternal estate—in **1740**. Again, for those of us born into meager means, any time some man or woman came into the world in an estate with its own name, we tend to assume that person is rich.

With regard to that belief, 𝔚𝔦𝔩𝔩𝔦𝔞𝔪 𝔓𝔞𝔠𝔞 did not disappoint. He was indeed born into one of the wealthier families in Maryland, and like those of his eventual fellow co-signers to the Declaration, wanted for nothing in life.

A side note on that point, but one that bears repeating as it helps to highlight the principles, patriotism, and courage of those among 𝔗𝔥𝔢 **56** with means, is that the vast majority of the others within the colonies who had or came from a very comfortable existence or great wealth were Loyalists siding with the Crown.

Many to most of them were, in fact, very good people. But "good people" who did not want to rock the boat, bring any attention to themselves, or, most importantly, endanger the vast sums of money they were taking in from the Crown.

Two thousand and twenty-two years ago, it was "thirty pieces of silver" that helped to ensure the betrayal of a cause and a "revolutionary."

In the mid- to late 1700s, that payoff jumped to millions.

Today, in 2022, tens to hundreds of billions of dollars are ensuring the inaction of "good people" who could stop the groupthink totalitarianism that is bringing about the suicide of the Republic 𝕿𝖍𝖊 56 envisioned and created.

Going back to the quote from the Benjamin Franklin Gates character in the movie *National Treasure*:

> ...if there's something wrong, those who have the ability to take action *have the responsibility to take action*.

Clearly, in and around 1765, countless "good people" knew there was something terribly wrong: that the British Crown was, in fact, cutting off all oxygen to the colonies. They also knew they had "the ability to take action" but still chose to turn their backs on their "responsibility to take action."

Why? Again, money, comfort, and self-interest. Each made the personal decision to ignore the oppression and atrocities so as not to offend their Crown paymasters.

Flash ahead to today, to 2022.

As also highlighted at the beginning of this book, there are thousands of conservatives, Republicans, Libertarians, and people of traditional faith who collectively have over $1 trillion under their control.

"Good people" who know precisely what the totalitarian groupthink is doing to our nation.

"Good people" who have the means to create honest and nonbiased media outlets, colleges, science and medical centers, search engines, and entertainment platforms.

"Good people" who know that is the *only course of action* to prevent the suicide of our nation.

And yet...

As the famous quote attributed to **Edmund Burke**—the father of conservatism and friend of the American colonies during his tenure in the British Parliament—warned: "The only thing necessary for the triumph of Evil is for good men to do nothing."

Well...

"Good men" did nothing two thousand and twenty-two years ago.

"Good men" did nothing during the Revolutionary War.

"Good men" do nothing today.

Rest assured the Evil spawned by "doing nothing" eventually does lay waste to the "good men" who choose to look the other way while enriching themselves. One way or the other or, as some believe, in one existence or the other.

જી

Now, back to an actual very good man, **William Paca**. He was homeschooled on the family estate, and sometime before his fifteenth birthday he was accepted into the College of Pennsylvania, from which he graduated around 1759.

After college, he extended his education by studying law in Annapolis, began practicing his chosen career by the age of twenty-one, and married a young woman by the name of Mary Chew.

Before, during, and after this time, he was a contemporary and friend of the aforementioned Samuel Chase. While they both strongly believed in an independent America free of the Crown oppression, they were not two peas from the same pod.

As loud and combative as Chase could be on occasion, Paca was quiet, thoughtful, and strategic all the time. In many ways during those most uncertain of times, the two friends from similar backgrounds and ages complemented each other perfectly.

Like Chase, Paca knew the political path was the one to walk to help effect the change needed. As such, he was elected to the Maryland legislature in 1768; joined the Maryland Committee of Correspondence; and, along with his good friend Chase, organized the successful campaign against the "poll tax" levied by the royal governor. In 1774, he also was elected to the First Continental Congress.

After signing the Declaration of Independence and as the war with the Crown was becoming a reality, Paca spent thousands of his own dollars to help supply the American soldiers. More than that, he also volunteered with the Maryland Militia.

In 1782, William Paca was elected Governor of Maryland. In 1788 he was named to the state convention to ratify the new federal constitution.

Not surprisingly to anyone who knew him, the personal cause he chose to support and lobby for during the remainder of his life was the welfare of the veterans of the Revolutionary War.

William Paca passed in **1799** just days before his fifty-ninth birthday.

CHAPTER TWENTY-FOUR

Thomas Stone

Imagine signing the **Declaration of Independence** but then still striving months behind the scenes to find an option to work it out with Great Britain.

What?

Thomas Stone of Maryland did not have to imagine it because he lived it. Even though he was an early Patriot and saw the need for independence for the American colonies he truly dreaded the specter of a long, drawn-out, and bloody conflict.

The next seven years proved why Stone was correct to feel that way. The anticipation and talk of war never remotely projected the actual horrific carnage inflicted on the young humans tasked with the fight or those who loved and lost them.

Thomas Stone was born on his parents' estate in Charles County, Maryland, in 1743. While born into some money, Stone was quietly determined to grow that advantage.

He knew that to do so, he would have to attain some education and then pick the proper career. He parents supplied him with a part-time tutor while he was young. When he reached his teen years, young Stone became an apprentice with a very successful Annapolis attorney.

By the time he was twenty-one years of age, he was admitted to the bar and opened his own practice in Frederick, Maryland. Several years later, he found and married the love of his life, a young woman by the name of Margaret Brown with whom he would have three children.

Stone's determination, work ethic, and twin careers as both a farmer and a lawyer did, in fact, make him quite wealthy. But as he was finding financial comfort, his mind was becoming ever more troubled by the abusive tactics being employed against the colonies by the Crown.

Even as everything in the world seemed to be going right for him, Stone felt it was his duty to speak out in favor of those less fortunate than himself who were paying an increasingly steep price because of the punitive British policies.

As his Patriotic voice was gaining more and more favor in Maryland, he was elected to the Continental Congress in late 1774. Reluctant to leave his beloved wife and children behind, Stone still felt he had no choice but to travel to Philadelphia to add his soft and measured voice to the deliberations tilting the scale toward independence and...war.

Once there, while mostly silent of voice, he became deeply involved in committee work, including those responsible for drafting the **Articles of Confederation**.

After signing the Declaration, he returned to Maryland fearful for what would happen to his colony, his neighbors and friends, and most of all his wife and children.

Stone served in the Maryland legislature from 1777 to 1781. He was reelected to the Continental Congress in 1783, a session that saw him briefly serve as that body's president.

In 1787 he was elected to serve at the Constitutional Convention. Sadly, he declined the honor because of his wife's failing health. When his Margaret passed just a few months later of smallpox, Stone became a lost soul consumed by grief.

His grief grew into an unstoppable depression, which quickly began to eat away at his physical health. Also, on the advice of his doctor, Stone decided to sail to England as a way to distract his increasingly troubled mind.

While waiting to board his ship leaving from Alexandria, Virginia, in June 1787, **Thomas Stone** dropped dead where he stood. He was only forty-four years of age.

CHAPTER TWENTY-FIVE

Charles Carroll

𝕭ecause of the aforementioned movie *National Treasure*, the name of 𝕮harles 𝕮arroll rightfully became a bit more familiar to millions of Americans—at least while they were in the theater or watching the film from the comfort of their homes.

As nice as that mention was, Carroll's real life deserves much more attention than his being used as a prop to set up the next scene of the blockbuster movie.

His life *was* a movie, a life with multiple historical markers. Three of those being: he was the longest-lived signer; he was the only Roman Catholic signer; and he was arguably the *wealthiest* of all the signers.

More than all of that, he was a Patriot who could not wait to put his talent and considerable resources exactly where his mouth was. And at any given time, his mouth was calling for "armed resistance" against the Crown.

Carroll was born in Annapolis, Maryland, to a very prosperous family in 1737. As mentioned, a *Roman Catholic* family. And it was because of his faith and the faith of his family that young **Charles Carroll** first experienced *outright bigotry* and *discrimination*.

Catholics were not tolerated in Maryland at that time, and Carroll soon found out how far and how threatening some of his fellow colonists would go to make that point abundantly clear to him.

By the time Charles was eight years of age, his father thought it best to take him to France to be among that large Catholic population and finish his education in relative peace. Carroll remained in France until approximately 1757, when he moved to London to finalize his legal education.

In 1765, and after two decades out of the country, Charles Carroll returned, not only highly educated but quite sophisticated as well.

Once again, the detested Stamp Act moves center stage in the life of a signer. Carroll returned just in time to witness— and then join—the growing protests against that penal policy.

With the protests growing, Carroll felt the fire ignited within him would only remain lit and spread if he sought out other Patriots in the area.

But even in the midst of protest, love can still blossom. And so it did for **Charles Carroll**, when in 1768 he married Mary Darnall. Then, as he and his Mary began to have the first of their seven children, Carroll's mind went back to not only the bigotry and discrimination he experienced as a child but also the oppressive tactics he watched the Crown employ against the Catholics in Ireland, the ancestral homeland of his family.

Those memories created a one-two punch of resentment against bullying and bigotry, which Carroll decided would be best landed upon the hopefully glass jaw of the Crown oppressors.

With William Paca, Samuel Chase, and Thomas Stone, Carroll helped to devise a well-organized public relations campaign meant to inflame their fellow colonists against the Crown. This public relations campaign would see Carroll as the main author of the seemingly nonstop propaganda.

Anti-Crown after anti-Crown essays were printed in the local paper, each one anonymously signed by "The First Citizen."

Like Ben Franklin's Silence Dogood letters, the serious essays of The First Citizen began to not only stir the masses against Britain but also to create an atmosphere of appreciation for the words and the talents of the anonymous writer. These words began causing the people to implore the Maryland legislature to act on their behalf, but this body was more than happy to straddle the fence of indecision for as long as possible.

For that reason and others, Maryland did not send a delegation to the First Continental Congress. But by 1776, things were moving in a decidedly different direction.

In the spring of that year, the Continental Congress asked Benjamin Franklin, along with Charles Carroll, his cousin John Carroll, and Samuel Chase to travel north to urge the Canadians to support the colonies in their coming fight with the Crown. Of interest, one of the main reasons Charles Carroll and his cousin were included in the delegation was because of their Roman Catholic roots. It was believed that their Catholic faith might serve as a catalyst to help sway the French-Canadian Catholics to come down on the side of the colonies.

It did not.

Quite symbolically, on July 4, 1776, Charles Carroll was elected to the Second Continental Congress. By August 2, he was signing the Declaration of Independence.

After the large and flamboyant signature of 𝕵𝖔𝖍𝖓 𝕳𝖆𝖓𝖈𝖔𝖈𝖐, the method 𝕮𝖍𝖆𝖗𝖑𝖊𝖘 𝕮𝖆𝖗𝖗𝖔𝖑𝖑 chose to sign his name has also created some debate, questions, and speculation.

For he did not just sign: 𝕮𝖍𝖆𝖗𝖑𝖊𝖘 𝕮𝖆𝖗𝖗𝖔𝖑𝖑 But rather: 𝕮𝖍𝖆𝖗𝖑𝖊𝖘 𝕮𝖆𝖗𝖗𝖔𝖑𝖑 *of Carrollton*.

One of the oldest known explanations for this reports:

> The question naturally arises, Why did Mr. Carroll append to his signature the place of his residence, "Carrollton." It is said that when he wrote his name, a delegate near him suggested, that as he had a cousin of the name of Charles Carroll, in Maryland, the latter might be taken for him, and he (the Signer) escape attainder, or any other punishments that might fall upon the heads of the Patriots. Mr. Carroll immediately seized the pen, and wrote "of Carrollton" at the end of his name, exclaiming "They cannot mistake me now."[26]

By 1778, Carroll returned to Maryland to help form the state government. His public participation was far from over. For the next decade plus, he served the people of his state in both the state legislature and the United States Senate.

Even with all of that, Carroll still found the time to ride his horse daily, something he was doing regularly right up until about his ninety-third year on Earth.

𝕮𝖍𝖆𝖗𝖑𝖊𝖘 𝕮𝖆𝖗𝖗𝖔𝖑𝖑 passed in 1832 at a truly advanced ninety-five years of age.

Chapter Twenty-Six

George Wythe

ou taught **Thomas Jefferson**, you signed the **Declaration of Independence**, you were a legal scholar and a hero to countless of your fellow Americans—and then a shifty, useless nephew poisons and kills you for your fortune.

A Revolutionary reminder of the truism: *"You can pick your friends, but you can't pick your family."*

George Wythe was born in 1726 on his family's estate in Elizabeth City County, Virginia. He was born into some money, but then tragedy struck when his father passed when Wythe was but a small child.

Wythe's mother—like so many women of that time—was mentally tough, highly intelligent, and a natural leader. With the passing of her husband, the tutoring of young George fell to her. As she was quite proficient in the classics of the time, as well as the Latin language, she instilled a rock-solid foundation of education and culture in her son.

But then, when Wythe was but twenty-one years of age, she too passed. With her passing, some believe George Wythe entered a somewhat dark period of depression, which he chose to medicate with self-indulgence.

While he most certainly did go into a mental tailspin with her loss, he pulled himself out of it at some point by deciding to pour all his energy into the study of law. By 1746, he was not only admitted to the bar but was also gaining the reputation as an exceptional student and even better teacher of the law.

Around this same time, he married a woman by the name of Ann Lewis. Tragically, she too was taken from Wythe when she passed unexpectedly less than a year after they were married. Sometime after that, he met and married a woman by the name of Elizabeth Taliaferro. They had one child, who did not live beyond infancy.

Not yet out of his twenties and Wythe had lost his father, mother, a wife, and his only child. These losses came to convince Wythe that while life was indeed fickle, humans had a right to happiness, safety, and liberty while on Earth.

Believing that, he also knew that the political and ruling class would determine the fate of most in one way another. Because of that reality, Wythe got himself elected to the House of Burgessess in 1775, a political body he served in for over twenty years.

But beyond the political, Wythe deeply believed that education was a key to self-determination. He knew that dictators and tyrants always sought to keep the people ignorant as a way to control and deceive them. Wythe was determined to remove some of that tyrannical control by educating the next generation of colonial leaders.

And educate them he did. Among his students before and after his time at the College of William and Mary in

Williamsburg were future presidents **Thomas Jefferson** and **James Monroe**, as well as **John Marshall** and **Henry Clay**.

Wythe was elected to the Continental Congress in 1775, and while he did eventually sign the **Declaration of Independence** sometime in the fall of 1776, his heart and mind were forever concerned with the welfare of Virginia.

He not only helped to design the state seal, but he also held various state-level offices upon his return, including as speaker of the lower house and as a judge of the Virginia Court of Chancery.

As he was working nonstop to improve the lives of his neighbors and fellow colonists, his conscience was telling him that he was failing one group of people in desperate need of his help: the slaves of Virginia.

As a minor slave owner himself, Wythe was coming to hate the dehumanizing and obscene institution. That troubled conscience, as well as his long-time belief in right and wrong, demanded that he take action.

Not only did he free his own slaves, but he decided to start a private school free of charge to those who chose to attend. One of those students was a young black man who had lived on his estate as a slave by the name of Michael Brown.

Wythe not only grew to deeply care for the young man but also felt he had come to be like a son to him in a number ways. So much so, that Wythe decided to include young Michael Brown in his will.

And that momentous decision brings us back full circle to the shifty, useless nephew, a disgusting leech of a human being who lived at his uncle's home and hoped to inherit all his childless uncle's estate and fortune. When he learned of Wythe's plan to give some of his fortune to young Michael

Brown—and a former slave at that—the shifty, useless nephew became totally unhinged.

Soon thereafter, the nephew served his uncle, his uncle's housekeeper, and young Michael Brown three cups of coffee spiked with poison. Wythe and the young man who was becoming like a son to Wythe died from the poisoning. The housekeeper survived, but as she was a black woman, she was not allowed to testify against the shifty, useless, and now killer of a nephew, who got away with the crime.

George Wythe—the "teacher of future presidents"—was murdered in **1806** at eighty years of age.

Chapter Twenty-Seven

Benjamin Harrison

𝔚 hile we may be reluctant to admit it, many of us secretly don't like overachieving people or families. They need to stop being good at...*everything*. Their unbridled successes tend to make our relatively small life achievements look like the head of a pin in comparison. That in turn, makes us insecure, envious, and grumpy.

If you are one of "us," then the "Harrison" clan may get on your nerves a bit. One signed the 𝖉𝖊𝖈𝖑𝖆𝖗𝖆𝖙𝖎𝖔𝖓 𝖔𝖋 𝕴𝖓𝖉𝖊𝖕𝖊𝖓𝖉𝖊𝖓𝖈𝖊, and then that guy's son became our ninth president and then his great-grandson became our twenty-third president.

Seriously. Stop showing off.

𝕭𝖊𝖓𝖏𝖆𝖒𝖎𝖓 𝕳𝖆𝖗𝖗𝖎𝖘𝖔𝖓 was born in Charles City County, Virginia, around 1726. While he was born into comfort at the time, he was not born into great wealth.

As they did have a comfortable existence, young 𝕭𝖊𝖓𝖏𝖆𝖒𝖎𝖓's father wanted to ensure that his son would get an education at the College of William and Mary. And a good education he was getting right up until tragedy struck. In this, case, quite literally struck.

Benjamin's father and two of his sisters were struck by lightning and instantly killed while on the grounds of their estate in Berkley. **Benjamin** felt he had no choice but to drop out of college to take over the day-to-day running of the family estate and farm.

As he was doing so, some happiness appeared on the horizon to help balance the tragedy he experienced when he had the great good fortune to meet and then marry Elizabeth Bassett—the one-day mother of a future president of the United States.

Now with a wife and growing family, and as he took on the responsibilities of the family business, **Benjamin** began to pay more and more attention to not only the local politics that affected his business but also the larger politics between the Crown and the colonies. Troubled by what he was reading, he felt the only course of action was to get involved at the local level. He did so by becoming one of the youngest members ever elected to the House of Burgesses. Shortly thereafter, he began to excel at the business of politics, with his voice reaching more and more of the people.

One of the people his voice was reaching was the royal governor (the representative of the Crown), who worried that **Harrison** was becoming a bit *too popular* and a bit *too persuasive* to the masses with his warnings about the Crown's systematic "scheme" for enslaving the colonies.

The royal governor—like others loyal to the Crown—felt a disguised bribe in the form of a seat in the executive council would serve to silence Mr. **Harrison**. Guess again.

Harrison not so diplomatically declined the offer and proceeded to outline in great detail the Crown's various and growing oppressions of the colonies to an increasingly red-faced royal governor.

But while Harrison was strongly in the corner of the colonies, he also felt it was critical to put forth calm, well thought-out, and long-term solutions to the Crown's overreach. And it was on that score that Harrison and the famous—or "infamous" to the British—Patrick Henry crossed rhetorical swords.

While Harrison was all in favor of Henry's crowd-pleasing quote: "*Give me Liberty or give me Death*," he also felt that Henry could fly off the handle at times and lose focus of the greater goal. That goal, to Harrison's way of thinking, was independence from the Crown with the least amount of death and destruction as possible.

As such, and while a member of the House of Burgesses, Harrison refused to endorse Henry's resolutions advocating for organized civil disobedience as retaliation for the Stamp Act. Patrick Henry told Harrison in no uncertain terms how angry he was, but this time, the usually quiet and efficient Harrison gave it back just as good as he got. Eventually, both Patriots agreed to disagree on the issue and move on in unison for the greater good.

In 1774, Benjamin Harrison was elected to the First Continental Congress. By the spring of 1776, he found himself chairman of the body. As such, he got to oversee and direct a number of the debates running up to the adoption of the Declaration of Independence. A document he was proud to sign.

Approximately one year later, he felt it was time to go home to serve in the legislature of Virginia, where he also presided as speaker. Aside from his political duties, he also served in the Virginia Militia during the time that the traitor

Benedict Arnold invaded the colony as well as when British General Cornwallis marched through the area.

In 1781, Harrison was elected governor of Virginia and served three terms. He passed away in 1791 at sixty-five years of age.

CHAPTER TWENTY-EIGHT

Thomas Nelson Jr.

N̲ow, we come to the Founding Father and signer of the 𝔇eclaration of 𝔍ndependence who ordered his troops to fire upon his own home during the Battle of Yorktown when he was told that British redcoats were hiding within it.

Try telling your bank today that you blew up your own home in defense of your nation and see what happens.

𝔗homas 𝔑elson 𝔍r. was also born into great wealth in Yorktown, Virginia, on 𝔇ecember 26, 1738. In his mid-to-late teens, he was sent to England by his father to complete his education. 𝔑elson was enrolled in Cambridge University and graduated in 1761.

While he was in London, it was said that he had acquired an intense interest in the inner workings of the British Parliament and even was able to witness Prime Minister George Grenville offer up the hated Stamp Act—the overreach that set the table for the American Revolution—while he was there.

The introduction of that act, and the loudly positive reaction of the members of Parliament to something 𝔑elson knew would serve to cripple the colonies, helped to convince him that he would have to take an active part in the defense of his homeland as soon as he returned.

When he did return to Yorktown, he married Lucy Grymes. Together, they would go on to have thirteen children. In 1764, at just twenty-five years of age, he was elected to Virginia's House of Burgesses.

In August 1774, he was first elected to the Continental Congress and then was reelected two years later. During that time, he also used his own money to outfit and train a light calvary in the defense of his county.

As he settled into the Continental Congress, Nelson's voice became one of the loudest calling for complete separation from the Crown, and on August 2, 1776, he signed the Declaration of Independence.

The following year, at just about thirty-eight years of age, it is believed that Nelson suffered a stroke. His friends, colleagues, and family begged him to retire from public life for good at that point.

Nelson refused. And even in the face of several ministrokes after that, he reentered the fray against the Crown in an amazingly big way. As in, he was given the rank of brigadier general in the militia. A title, even though he was still quite weak at times, he took very seriously.

How seriously?

By the time the British invaded Virginia in 1781, Nelson had become not only the governor—succeeding Thomas Jefferson—but the commander in chief of the *entire* Virginia Militia. It should be noted, that when the militia was called from their homes, many families were left with nothing to survive on. General Nelson then personally donated what may have turned out to be the last of his own money to support over one hundred families as the battle loomed.

In the fall of that year, General Nelson led approximately 3,000 militia as a part of General George Washington's army at Yorktown. During the ensuing battle, it was learned that some of the British military leadership had taken over Nelson's personal home and were using it as a command post against the militiamen.

Nelson was outraged that the British would desecrate his home in such a manner and ordered his own forces to fire upon it and destroy it.

When they initially refused out of respect for him, he screamed: "Give me the Cannon."[27]

Realizing their general was serious, his men proceeded to fire their cannons at the Nelson home.

The British soon surrendered at Yorktown on October 19, 1781, signaling the end of the Revolutionary War. The war ultimately had taken a tremendous toll on Thomas Nelson Jr.

Once, one of the wealthier men in Virginia, he lost his fortune, sacrificed his health, and passed away in poverty at just fifty years of age in 1789.

CHAPTER TWENTY-NINE

Francis Lightfoot Lee

As the cliché—and the hit song by Lynn Anderson—reminds us: *"Still waters run deep."*

Few were deeper or more still than 𝔉rancis 𝔏ightfoot 𝔏ee. Especially when he had to operate in the shadow of his highly respected and Revolution-inspiring older brother 𝔕ichard 𝔥enry 𝔏ee.

Lee was born on 𝔒ctober 14, 1734, at Stratford Hall in Westmoreland County, Virginia. Unlike his worldly older brother Richard, 𝔉rancis was educated at home and became somewhat of a homebody, comfortable in that environment.

The Lee family wanted for nothing, and 𝔉rancis was quite content to lead a life of privilege until that same life forced him to grow up and pick a side.

While he truly loved and admired his older brother Richard, after his marriage to Rebecca Taylor and once 𝔉rancis himself entered the House of Burgesses, he morphed into a confidant of one of our nation's most famous orators, Patriots, and...troublemakers. That person being 𝔓atrick 𝔥enry.

Even though Lee was two years older than Henry, Francis felt they had more than a few things in common, which made him quite comfortable in the presence of someone—very much like his brother—who could be larger than life at times.

Like him, Francis knew that it had taken Henry some time to find his way in life as an adult. Henry had to work as a tavernkeeper in his father-in-law's inn while teaching himself law before finally opening his own law practice in 1760.

Like him, Francis knew it had taken a while for Henry to find his soon-to-be-famous voice and his unique identity—a voice that was really announced to the Crown and the world in March 1775 when the Second Virginia Convention met at St. John's Church in Richmond, Virginia, to discuss the direction to take against an ever-more-aggressive oppressor.

It was at that event, that Lee knew Patrick Henry had thrown down his gauntlet with his impassioned speech, close to one of the most famous speeches in the history of the United States. Said Henry to sum up his thoughts regarding the Crown's abuse of the colonies:

> Gentlemen may cry, "Peace, Peace," but there is no peace. The war is actually begun! The next gale that sweeps from the north will bring to our ears the clash of resounding arms! Our brethren are already in the field! Why stand we here idle?… Is life so dear, or peace so sweet, as to be purchased at the price of chains and slavery? Forbid it, Almighty God! I know not what course others may take; but as for me, **give me liberty, or give me death!** [28] [Emphasis mine]

Francis Lightfoot Lee truly and deeply agreed with Henry. More than that, he knew that to side with such a powerful voice within the resistance would give him an identity that was not attached to or handed down from his continually celebrated older brother.

Comfortable in the role he had carved out for himself, Lee moved on with his life in peace. He was sent to the Continental Congress in 1775 and chose to let his work on various committees—including helping to draft the Articles of Confederation—do his speaking for him.

On July 2, 1776, Lee voted for the Declaration of Independence and on August 2, he signed the document he knew was giving life to a new nation.

In 1779, he retired from the Continental Congress to return to Virginia to serve in the senate for a time before retiring entirely from public life. During that retirement, he continued to use his wealth to help family, friends, and neighbors in need.

Francis Lightfoot Lee passed in 1797 at sixty-two years of age. His beloved wife, Rebecca, passed but a few days after him. All who knew them said she died of a "broken heart."

CHAPTER THIRTY

Carter Braxton

Stop me if you have heard this one before. Carter Braxton was born into a very wealthy landowning family.

But once again, that is also the counterintuitive point that should be made again and again regarding these 56 truly remarkable men. The vast majority of the wealthy in the colonies were Loyalists to the Crown, anxious to bow and scrape before their British oppressors rather than risk losing one pence or their social status among the elite of the land.

Signing their names to a document that would cause the Crown to hunt them down like rabid animals was a risk that never entered their privileged and pampered minds. Once again, much better to hide under a bench in the stands whimpering than step into that arena to fight for liberty, dignity, and life.

Surely, these rich and pompous colonists thought, *the poor, unwashed masses among us who do our daily bidding will also risk their lives to protect our great wealth and endless property.*

How shocked those elitist cowards must have been when tens of men with as much or more money as them stepped from the shadows directly into the arena to scream across an ocean at London: "We will suffer your indignities and oppression no more. Today, we fight for our rights as human beings. Rights handed down from God."

Carter Braxton was one of those tens of wealthy men who proclaimed: "I stand with the American people against the tyranny of the Crown."

The fact that it took him some time to come to that Revolutionary point of view had nothing to do with capitulating to the British and everything to do with his hatred of war and the loss of precious human life.

Carter Braxton was born on **September 10, 1736**, at then-Newington in King and Queen County, Virginia. He lost his mother while he was but a small child and his very wealthy father but a decade later.

He and his brother were then taken in by family, who raised them as their own. Braxton graduated from the College of William and Mary and at nineteen years of age proceeded to marry Judith Robinson, the daughter of one of the wealthier families in the area.

Quite tragically, Judith passed at not quite twenty-one years of age while giving birth to their second child. Devastated by the loss of his wife, young **Braxton** set sail for England to distract his mind from the sorrow in Virginia.

Upon his return to America a few years later, he met and married a young woman by the name of Elizabeth Corbin.

Now, while **Samuel Adams** might be known as the "Father of the Revolution," **Carter Braxton** could lay claim to being the "Father of Posterity." For by the time he was done, he had fathered a total of eighteen children.

By 1761, Braxton was elected to the House of Burgesses. All was pretty quiet and routine for him for the next fourteen years as he led a life of leisure while dealing with some of the more mundane political issues before him.

Then came April 20, 1775. It was the day after the red-coats had marched into Lexington and Concord. This triggering event prompted Virginia's royal Governor, Lord John Dunmore, to seize the gunpowder in the Williamsburg magazine. That move inflamed the leaders of several Virginia Militia units. One of them led by…who else? Patrick Henry.

Cooler heads tried to prevail, and all but one of the militia units were convinced to hold off on any military action. The one not backing down, naturally, was being led by the rabble-rouser Henry, who marched his Hanover County troops straight on into Williamsburg.

As hostilities were about to commence, Carter Braxton offered to act as a go-between for Henry with the royal governor. Henry accepted the offer for one simple reason. He knew that Braxton's father-in-law was acting as the representative for the royal governor, and, therefore, if anyone could walk away from the table with a deal, it would be Braxton.

Patrick Henry had demanded either the return of the gunpowder or payment for it from the royal governor in exchange for him and his militia not attacking. Braxton was able to convince his father-in-law that Henry would indeed attack. That conviction forced his father-in-law to agree to pay for the gunpowder and avert certain bloodshed.

In the fall of that same year, Braxton was selected to fill a vacancy in the Continental Congress caused by the sudden passing of Peyton Randolph. Upon his arrival in Philadelphia in early 1776, Braxton was still far from convinced that forcing independence from the Crown—and certain war—was a prudent plan of action. But during extended and sometimes heated discussions and debates with his fellow delegates, Braxton came to believe that independence and true liberty were the only answers.

Like a number of other signers, Braxton put his money where his mouth was and lent a great deal of his personal fortune for the purchase of supplies for the American forces. That generosity combined with the British capturing most of his vessels and destroying his estate and landholding ruined him financially.

A man who grew up in great wealth, signed the Declaration of Independence, and donated much of his money to the war effort while losing all of his possessions to British vengeance, was soon—quite shamefully—being threatened with being sent to "debtors' prison."

Before that humiliation could become a reality, Carter Braxton passed away in 1797 at sixty-one years of age.

CHAPTER THIRTY-ONE

Robert Morris

𝕬 question for legitimate debate is this: Which ultimately is more important—being the "Father of the Revolution" or being the "Financier of the Revolution?"

If the vote is for the latter, then the trophy goes to **Robert Morris** of Pennsylvania. For if an army does indeed "march on its stomach," then Morris was the main force behind keeping the Continental Army fed, clothed, supplied, and...armed.

Morris was born in Lancashire, England, in January **1734**. His father was a merchant businessman extensively engaged with the Americas in trade. As such, he moved to the Maryland area to better facilitate his growing business.

When **Robert** was thirteen years old, his father sent for him and the rest of the family to come live with him there. Soon thereafter, he sent **Robert** to a school in Philadelphia.

As a young teen, **Robert** quickly realized that he was very good with numbers, mathematics, and the equations of the financial world. As such, by **1754**—after apprenticing with **Charles Willing**, one of the leading merchants in the city— **Morris** formed a mercantile business partnership with one of Willing's sons upon the passing of the elder Willing. This partnership soon made both men two of the wealthiest people in Philadelphia.

For twenty years **Morris** grew his business, married Mary White in 1769, and enjoyed his life as one of the upper crust of the blossoming colonial city. But then, the impending Revolution demanded the attention of the man who was a "wizard" with numbers. He would give that attention and so much more.

Morris was elected to the Continental Congress in 1775. Very much like **Carter Braxton** and a few of the other 56, **Morris** had his doubts with regard to complete independence from the mother country. His doubts remarkably still lived on even *after* he signed the **Declaration of Independence**.

But once those doubts were permanently erased, **Morris** jumped into the Revolution like a man possessed. He knew that—because of his unique and unrivaled financial gifts—the responsibility to fund the Revolution rested with him.

Because of his obvious financial skills, the Continental Congress named him the head of the "Secret Committee," the committee tasked solely with financing the fight against the Crown. As the finances of the colonies and the Continental Army were in tatters, **Morris** had his work cut out for him.

Not only did **Morris** leverage his considerable wealth to help fund the War of Independence, but he badgered the colonies and every wealthy colonist he knew to help rescue the newly declared Republic's collapsed finances.

With the unlimited power granted him by the Continental Congress—combined with his now sacred mission—**Morris** truly was our nation's very first "secretary of the Treasury."

Just how important did **Robert Morris** become to the eventual victory of the Continental Army? In a word: "Everything."

As was reported over 175 years ago:

> Even when the American army under Washington, had dwindled down to a handful of half-naked, half-famished militia, during the disastrous retreat across New Jersey at the close of 1776, he evinced his confidence that final success would ensue, by loaning at that time, upon his individual responsibility, ten thousand dollars. This materially assisted in collecting together and paying that gallant band with which Washington re-crossed the Delaware, and won the glorious victory at Trenton.[29]

In 1781, he somehow managed to combine a loan from France with—again—some of his own money to finance both the Yorktown campaign and a new national bank, called at the time the Bank of North America. This new bank not only created confidence in the new American system but also established a line of credit with other nations.

In 1787, **Morris** found himself a delegate to the Constitutional Convention. Again, of note, he and Roger Sherman were the only two of **The 56** to sign both the **Declaration of Independence**, the **Articles of Confederation**, and the **United States Constitution**.

In 1789, **Morris** turned down the honor of serving as the nation's official secretary of the Treasury. He did so to serve in the United States Senate. Six years later, **Morris** chose to retire from public life, having literally given his all for his new nation.

And just *how* was he rewarded for his immeasurable contributions to the Revolution and American Independence? In 1798, he was sent to debtors' prison in Philadelphia because of business deals gone bad after he had lost all of his wealth in service to his new nation.

Yes, you read that correctly.

To the everlasting shame of all those who incarcerated him, the man who financed the very liberty of the United States of America spent over three years in prison.

When Robert Morris was finally released, he was a broken man and died in squalor in 1806 at seventy-two years of age. His imprisonment is a stain on our nation that should never be forgiven or forgotten.

CHAPTER THIRTY-TWO

Benjamin Rush

There were a number of things one could do around the time of the American Revolution to sully one's reputation and ignite a firestorm of hate by fellow colonists, but being part of a secret cabal to remove General George Washington from his command had to be right at the top of that list.

Benjamin Rush was born on December 24, 1745, about twelve miles northeast of Philadelphia. After his father passed when he was just six years of age, he and his siblings were left close to poverty in the care of their mother.

Fortunately for them, she was an incredibly intelligent, competent, and soon-to-be-accomplished woman. Realizing she could no longer care for her children on the small farm she could not manage, she sold it and used the little money she got to move to Philadelphia and open a small store, which soon became a real success thanks entirely to her initiative, skill, and determination.

As she ran the store, it became quite evident to her that her son Benjamin had been gifted by God with a truly exceptional mind. Knowing that, she felt it was her duty to expand that mind with the best education she could provide. That determined, the brilliant young Rush entered the College of New Jersey and received his degree at just sixteen years of age.

Not satisfied with that accomplishment, he got himself appointed as an apprentice to a very prominent doctor in Philadelphia. After getting some experience under his belt, Rush felt it best to head back to England to continue his education. In 1768 he enrolled at the University of Edinburgh, where he earned his full medical degree.

After spending some time traveling about London and Paris, Rush felt it best to return home to the colonies. Once back in Philadelphia, he opened a private medical practice while almost simultaneously being appointed as a professor of chemistry at the College of Philadelphia. Although he had paying patients, Rush went out of his way—and at his own expense—to treat the poor of the city free of charge.

Almost immediately upon his return—most especially because of the talk and threats against the colonies he heard while in London—now Dr. Rush made it known to as many as possible, that he was strongly in favor of independence for the colonies.

In 1776, two momentous occasions marked his life. The first was that he did in fact become a member of the Continental Congress and was able to sign the Declaration of Independence. With regard to that signing, it was reported that Dr. Rush observed:

> Awful silence pervaded the house when we
> were called up, one after the other, to the table
> of the President of the Congress to subscribe
> (sign) what was believed by many at that time,
> to be our own death warrants.[30]

Indeed, it was.

The second momentous occasion was that **Rush** married a young woman by the name of Julia Stockton. As fate and coincidence would have it, she was the daughter of fellow Declaration signer **Richard Stockton**.

By 1777, Dr. **Rush** became the surgeon general of the Continental Army—quite an honor and an even more daunting responsibility.

Unfortunately, during the course of his duties with the Army, **Rush** became convinced—along with a number of others—that **General George Washington** was over his head as commander of the Army and should be replaced.

Toward that end, a secret cabal was created to bring about that desired outcome. This cabal included highly decorated General Gates, **Rush,** and an overly ambitious foreign officer by the name of **Thomas Conway**. Thus, the group came to be known as the "Conway Cabal."

To be sure, like any commander or military officer, **General Washington** had his ups and downs while on the field of battle. Some downs were a matter of happenstance, while a few were indeed of his own making. That said, Washington was already considered to be a supreme hero to the colonies and to plot against him in secret was a real risk to reputation and even life.

Then, with swift military precision, **General Washington** proceeded to cut down his main rhetorical accuser. Said Washington in part of **Conway**:

> General Conway's merit, then, as an Officer, and his importance in this Army, exist more in his own imagination than in reality…[31]

Ouch.

With Washington's subsequent military victories, the cabal dissipated, and those publicly associated with it were held in scorn by many Americans. **Benjamin Rush** was one so held in scorn for his involvement in the group.

Either by plan or simply by the brilliance of his work, Dr. **Rush** repaired the damage to his reputation over the coming years by becoming the "Father of American Medicine." He especially demonstrated his courage and commitment to the ill when a wave of yellow fever decimated the population of Philadelphia in 1793. Many of the local doctors became understandably alarmed for their own safety and that of their families, and fled the city.

Dr. **Rush** refused to leave. With some of his colleagues and even medical students, he stayed to treat the sick and the dying. While doing so, he himself was attacked by the fever.

Said Dr. **Rush** to those colleagues and students:

> As for myself, I am determined to remain. I may fall a victim to the epidemic, and so may you, gentlemen. But I prefer, since I am placed here by Divine Providence, to fall in performing my duty, if such must be the consequence of staying upon the ground, than to secure my life by fleeing from the Post of Duty allotted in the Providence of God, I will remain, if I remain alone.[32]

Wow. All rhetorical sins against **George Washington** forgiven.

Aside from his exceptional medical and teaching skills, **Rush** was also a staunch advocate for the abolition of slavery, for the education of women and the poor, and even for prison reform. In many ways, he was truly ahead of his time.

Before **Dr. Benjamin Rush** passed in **1813** at the age of sixty-seven, he had educated over 3,000 medical students. Remarkable.

CHAPTER THIRTY-THREE

John Morton

Among this accomplished and heroic list of **56 Signers**, it would be natural to aspire to be first among equals in at least some notable way. **John Morton** achieved that designation, but it was in a category he would have much preferred to come in last.

He was the first to pass away and did not live a full year after signing the **Declaration of Independence**.

Morton was born in then Chester County, Pennsylvania, in 1725. Sadly, his father did not live to see his birth, and when his mother remarried later, **Morton** was raised by a very well-educated Englishman, who was a surveyor by trade and instructed his stepson in all things mathematics.

Because of his stepfather, **Morton** himself became a surveyor while also tending to the family farm. However, as much as he enjoyed the work, his passion for politics soon began to consume his mind and his time.

Even after his marriage to Ann Justis and the birth of his children, **Morton** could not get local or even international politics out of his mind. Because of that permanent interest, he got himself elected to the Pennsylvania state legislature in 1756, a political body he served in for the remainder of his natural life.

In addition to that, he served as both a justice of the peace and a sheriff for his county. For **Morton**, the more political and personal interaction with the people, the better.

In 1774, he reached two impressive milestones: his appointment as an associate justice of the Pennsylvania Supreme Court, and much more important—at least for the purposes of this project—his selection to the First Continental Congress.

And within that congress, it was his vote that helped to set history in motion. For it was **John Morton** who cast the deciding vote that placed Pennsylvania in favor of independence.

As was reported several decades later:

> By virtue of his previous election, Mr. Morton was in his seat on the memorable fourth of July, 1776. The delegation from Pennsylvania then present were equally divided in opinion upon the subject of independence, and Mr. Morton was called upon officially to give a casting vote for that State. This was a solemn responsibility thrown upon him—it was for him to decide whether there should be a unanimous vote of the Colonies for Independence— whether Pennsylvania should form one of the American Union. Be he firmly met the responsibility, and voted YES; and from that moment the United Colonies were declared Independent States…[33]

While Morton did indeed proudly fulfill that "solemn responsibility," he did pay a very high price for his Patriotism.

His passion for politics had always been most rewarding to him when he was helping the people of his beloved Chester County. But there was one insurmountable problem with that joy: the vast majority of the population of Chester County were Loyalists to the Crown. Upon his return from signing the Declaration, many of his friends and neighbors not only abandoned him but also labeled him a traitor.

No matter their scorn, John Morton proclaimed to anyone who would still listen to him that his signing of that document had been: "The most glorious service I ever rendered my country."[34]

He passed away on April 1, 1777, at fifty-two years of age—just nine months after casting the deciding vote for Pennsylvania and signing the Declaration of Independence.

Chapter Thirty-Four

George Clymer

As life and real-world experience have taught most of us, becoming an orphan at a very young age usually leads to a brutal existence for said orphan.

But, as we have also learned with regard to a few of the **56 Signers**, sometimes after you become an orphan, you get catapulted into great wealth. Such was the case for **George Clymer**.

Clymer was born in Philadelphia in **1739**. His mother passed away when he was but an infant, and then his father passed when **George** was just seven years of age. But, as we discovered with **John Hancock**, sometimes good fortune can ride to the rescue in the persons of a loving uncle and aunt.

The uncle who took **Clymer** in was indeed quite prosperous from having run a very successful mercantile business for years. While his uncle endeavored to bring him into the business, at least as a teen, **Clymer**'s main passions were literature and science.

Ironically, but quite understandably, it was the love of a good woman that brought him into the mercantile business. At around twenty-six years of age, **George** met and married a woman by the name of Elizabeth Meredith. As fate would have it, *her father* also ran a very successful mercantile business, a business George seemed to have no trouble jumping into after giving his own uncle the brush-off.

Did pressure from his new wife or a judgmental father-in-law play a role in Clymer suddenly deciding that was the business for him? While history does not quite spell it out, it has been known to happen that way.

Regardless of why he went into the business, he was soon part of "Meredith and Sons." Sadly, soon after he joined, his uncle passed away. Not so sadly for Clymer, his uncle left him the majority of his fortune.

While not really needing to work after his large inheritance, George still decided to stay at Meredith and Sons. When his father-in-law passed away, Clymer partnered with his brother-in-law to run the company.

Around the same time as his marriage, the Stamp Act was introduced, an act that infuriated Clymer. As such, he also became one of the first prominent Philadelphians to support total independence from the Crown.

With each passing month and year, his opposition to the edicts of the Crown was becoming more vocal and more tinged with rage. With that resentment bouncing about his mind, come 1773 he led a committee that forced the resignation of the Philadelphia tea consignees appointed by the Crown under the Tea Act.

Three years later, he was elected to the Second Continental Congress. Aside from eagerly signing the Declaration of Independence, he also served as one of the two Continental treasurers.

But as we have outlined, signing that document made 𝔗𝔥𝔢 56 men hunted prey for the vengeful redcoat army. 𝕮𝖑𝖞𝖒𝖊𝖗 was no exception.

As was reported:

> After the defeat of the Americans at the Brandywine, and the British were marching triumphantly toward Philadelphia, Mr. Clymer moved his family into the country for safety. But their retreat was discovered, and the British Soldiers sacked the house, destroyed the furniture, and wasted every sort of property which they could find.[35]

The destruction of his home and all his material wealth only served to strengthen 𝕮𝖑𝖞𝖒𝖊𝖗's resolve to attain independence for the colonies. Jumping back into that mission, part of 𝕮𝖑𝖞𝖒𝖊𝖗's duties were to help manage Indian affairs for the colonies.

In 1787 he was elected as a delegate to the Constitutional Convention and became one of the few signers of both the Declaration and the United States Constitution.

As one of the members who helped 𝕽𝖔𝖇𝖊𝖗𝖙 𝕸𝖔𝖗𝖗𝖎𝖘 to create the first national bank for the colonies, 𝕮𝖑𝖞𝖒𝖊𝖗 put that experience to work by accepting an appointment from then 𝕻𝖗𝖊𝖘𝖎𝖉𝖊𝖓𝖙 𝕲𝖊𝖔𝖗𝖌𝖊 𝖂𝖆𝖘𝖍𝖎𝖓𝖌𝖙𝖔𝖓 in 1791 to serve as the United States tax collector for Pennsylvania. Three years later, he was still serving in that role when the infamous tax revolt known as the "Whiskey Rebellion" broke out.

Quite ironically in the face of the Stamp Act serving as a catalyst for the outbreak of the American Revolution, the

Whiskey Rebellion was an organized uprising of farmers and distillers in Western Pennsylvania who were protesting a whiskey tax foisted upon them by the new federal government.

After years of protest against this tax, emotions finally exploded into outright confrontation, and the first president of the United States had to send in federal troops to crush what he feared might be a revolution against the leadership of the new Republic.

Not only was the Whiskey Rebellion seen as the first major test for the new American government, but it also served as a tipping point to help push Washington's Federalist Party out of power come 1802.

Tragically for **George Clymer**, he lost one of his sons to that long, drawn-out, and very ugly rebellion. It was that loss that convinced him that he needed to make a retreat from public life, something he did in 1796.

But with his retirement from public life, he jumped right back into the business and cultural world with both feet. He did so by serving as the very first president of the Philadelphia bank, the first president of the Philadelphia Academy of Fine Arts, and as vice president of the Philadelphia Agricultural Society.

Grief and personal loss aside, **George Clymer** was determined to leave the world a better place than when he found it. He passed away in 1813 at seventy-three years of age.

Chapter Thirty-Five

James Smith

There were some fairly unique personalities among the **56 Signers**, so to be thought of as "eccentric" by that bunch would be saying something.

James Smith was born in Ireland right around **1720**. He and his family moved to York County, Pennsylvania, when he was about ten years of age.

While **Smith**'s family did not have a great deal of money, they were comfortable and able to send him to the College of Philadelphia. After leaving school, he studied law in his brother's office before setting out on his own to practice law in the frontier country of Cumberland County.

Unfortunately for **James**, because it was "frontier country," there was not much legal business to be had, which forced him to relocate back to York, where his legal work picked up considerably.

Sometime around **1761** he met and married Eleanor Armor. They would eventually have five children together, but only one would live long enough to reach adulthood.

That tragic fact brings us back to **Smith**'s reputation for being eccentric. As anyone who has lost children, siblings, or parents way before their time knows, the human mind deals with grief in very unique and often protective ways. Many times, just below the surface of nonstop joking and eccentric behavior is a bottomless pit of sorrow and grief.

As was once observed, if each of us could take our most personal of problems and pile them atop each other in the Sahara Desert, we would look at all the other heart-wrenching misery before us and quickly and gladly grab our personal problem and run back home.

Sometimes "happy waters" run much deeper than still waters.

Going back to **James Smith**, right around the time of his marriage, he also started to become a bit of a political leader in his area. By 1774, he was much more comfortable offering his opinion regarding the oppressions of the Crown and possible responses from the colonies. So much so that he wrote and offered up a paper he titled "Essay on the Constitutional Power of Great Britain over the Colonies in America."

Within the body of that very thoughtful—and provocative—work, **Smith** dared to suggest two "Revolutionary" courses of action. The first one was a general boycott of all British goods. The second, and much more impressive, suggestion was the creation of a "general congress" for the colonies.

With regard to his own home area, he created a volunteer militia unit for York, a unit that elected him as its leader. That in and of itself proved to be a wise move, as **Smith** soon grew the militia to over battalion size, with as many as 20,000 men.

Smith was appointed to the Provincial Convention in Philadelphia in 1775. One year later, he was helping to draft the Pennsylvania state constitution. That same year, he was elected to the Continental Congress and signed the Declaration of Independence on August 2, 1776.

While it is not covered in our history as much as it should be—and never will be if some succeed in eradicating all "offensive" American history—Smith's hometown of York actually served as the temporary capital of the Revolution for a few months when the Continental Congress had to flee Philadelphia as the British redcoats marched on the city with the intention of rounding up those who dared to sign the Declaration.

While the Continental Congress was located in York, Smith provided his private office to be used for the meetings of the Board of War.

In 1782, he was appointed a brigadier general of the Pennsylvania Militia. While he was greatly honored to be so chosen, he felt because of his "advanced age" the title should go to a younger soldier.

Once that decision was made, he happily turned his attention back to his law practice in York along with the company of his friends and family.

The always happy, always joking, always eccentric James Smith passed away in 1806 at about eighty-seven years of age.

Chapter Thirty-Six

George Taylor

Imagine wanting to come to the Americas so badly that you would agree to become an indentured servant to accomplish that goal.

George Taylor did not have to imagine it as that was the contract he signed in order to have his passage paid for to the New World, a fee he would have to work off before being released from his indentured obligations.

Who knew that once he got to the Philadelphia area, his life would turn into a bit of a late-night soap opera?

Taylor was born in Ireland in 1716. Twenty years later, upon his arrival in the Philadelphia area, he found himself working off his passage paid for by Mr. Savage, who was an ironmaster at Warwick Furnace in Chester County.

Realizing that Taylor was fairly bright and industrious, Mr. Savage soon promoted him from menial labor in the factory to a bookkeeper for the company. Sometime after that, things became very intriguing, to say the least, and might make for a very entertaining movie for cable television or streaming.

Mr. Savage—the man who paid for Taylor's passage and then promoted him from the backbreaking work around the insufferable heat of the furnaces—suddenly passed away. When he did, he left behind a very attractive widow by the name of Anne.

While some at the time believed that George Taylor and Anne Savage may have had a bit of a "history" before her husband died, the fact of the matter is that soon after he did pass away, Taylor married his widow, Anne. Along with marrying Mr. Savage's widow, Taylor also got to take over Mr. Savage's company.

Uh, okay.

Soon thereafter, the former indentured servant was becoming very wealthy. So wealthy, in fact, that he felt his wife, Anne—with whom he quickly had two children—should have a housekeeper to help her with the chores about the home. As it turned out, the housekeeper Taylor selected was a very attractive young woman by the name of Naomi Smith—a woman who, some accounts tell us, provided Taylor with an additional five children on the side.

"Hello, Hollywood."

Taylor's gossip-producing life took a more public turn when in 1747 he took a commission as a captain in the Chester County Militia.

From that moment on, he seemed to adopt a more serious and responsible manner. It turned out that he truly did like to help the people of his area—so much so that he was soon appointed a justice of the peace for Bucks County and then a justice of the peace and a representative in the legislature for Northampton County.

Growing into his newfound responsibilities, **Taylor** served six years in the provincial assembly of Pennsylvania, worked on the Committees of Correspondence and Safety, and was promoted to a colonel for the militia representing Bucks and Northampton Counties.

In 1776, he was elected to the Second Continental Congress and signed the **Declaration of Independence** on **August 2**, 1776.

Some felt that because he did come to the Americas as an indentured servant **Taylor** always had a chip on his shoulder and was always ready for a fight. Whether or not he did have that chip, he was continually, strongly, and quite vocally in favor of independence from the Crown. Because he was also a military officer, he realized that his greatest contribution to the war effort would be the production of ordnance for the Continental Army from his Durham Furnace factory. And produce it, he did.

Unfortunately for **Taylor**, the new and still impoverished government basically stiffed him on paying a fair price for the massive amount of ordnance he did supply. Because of that, in 1778 he lost his factory to, of all things, to a Philadelphia Loyalist to the Crown.

George Taylor passed away at sixty-five years of age in 1781.

CHAPTER THIRTY-SEVEN

James Wilson

Once again, imagine signing the **Declaration of Independence**, being the second-most influential voice regarding the need for and creation of the Constitution, and becoming one of the very first justices of the US Supreme Court and your reward from a grateful nation is to have you thrown into debtors' prison...twice.

Born in Scotland in 1742, **James Wilson** came to America right around 1766. Educated at the University of Edinburgh, he began his career in his newly adopted country as a teacher.

Soon thereafter, he decided that the study and practice of law would be better suited to his needs. Once proficient in that field, he was admitted to the bar in Philadelphia in 1767 and moved to Carlisle, Pennsylvania, where he established a very successful practice.

About that same time, he met and then married Rachel Bird. **James** and Rachel went on to have six children.

Also, about that same time, he was becoming and more involved in the Revolutionary cause against the Crown. Truth be told, because he was from Scotland, he did not need any persuading, as he had both witnessed and heard of various Crown atrocities committed in his former homeland.

With his anti-Crown credentials now firmly established, in 1774, Wilson joined the local Committee of Correspondence. More than that, he himself authored a widely read pamphlet in which he made the case that the Crown had no right to impose laws upon the colonies.

In large part because of that, he was elected to the Continental Congress in 1775 and signed the Declaration of Independence the next year.

After that, he engaged in a number of professional and business activities—most quite honorable; a few, fraught with bad business decisions. On the "honorable" side, for a few years, he served as an advocate general for France in the Americas. Simultaneously, he counterintuitively decided to offer paid legal advice to Loyalists and their sympathizers.

Again…what?

One theory as to why he did so was because he was desperately in need of money as his own personal finances had collapsed because of his own bad choices with regard to land speculation.

Quite strangely, even though he had made a complete mess of his own finances, he was still able to somehow help Robert Morris in both the creation of the Bank of North America and the resolution of his new nation's more precarious financial problems.

By 1787, Wilson had been elected to the Constitutional Convention. It was there that he truly found his sweet spot. For not only did he excel in helping to draft the document, but he also became a highly respected orator during the floor debates.

Two years later, **President George Washington** appointed Wilson to the United States Supreme Court. Sadly, soon after that, his life spiraled out of control because of suspicious business deals—business deals that not only soon saw him broke but also incarcerated in debtors' prison because he could no longer pay his bills.

His time in prison, combined with the physical and mental fatigue it caused, rendered **James Wilson** unemployable. He passed away in 1798 just two weeks shy of his fifty-sixth birthday.

CHAPTER THIRTY-EIGHT

George Ross

Just exactly *how* does a Loyalist to the oppressive Crown get elected to the Continental Congress? Could a famous niece by the name of 𝕭𝖊𝖙𝖘𝖞 𝕽𝖔𝖘𝖘 have anything to do with it?

𝕲𝖊𝖔𝖗𝖌𝖊 𝕽𝖔𝖘𝖘 was born in New Castle, Delaware, in 1730. His father was a Scotland-born Episcopal minister, who moved his family to Pennsylvania after being made the assistant rector of the then-famous Christ Church in Philadelphia.

𝕽𝖔𝖘𝖘's very spiritual father was a stickler for a classical education and made sure young George became proficient in both Greek and Latin. Once he was in his teens, both George and his father thought it best that he continue his education at his older brother's law office in Philadelphia.

Having done so, 𝕽𝖔𝖘𝖘 was admitted to the bar in 1750 and proceeded to establish his own law practice in Lancaster. As luck and fate would have it, one of his very first clients happened to be an extremely beautiful young woman by the name of Anne Lawler. Proving that he did receive a first-rate education and was indeed quite intelligent, George asked Anne to marry him in 1751. She happily agreed, and they went on to have three children together.

From 1751 until about 1763, Ross also served as the Crown prosecutor for Cumberland County. It was during that time that his loyalties seemed to be tied more to Great Britain than to the colonies.

From 1768 to 1775, Ross was part of the provincial legislature. It was there that he was first really exposed to the growing conflict between the colonies and the Crown. That said, during that time, his personal scale of justice still seemed to be tipping in favor of England, a reality that was beginning to infuriate a number of his fellow members.

More problematic for Ross was the fact that he had also been elected to the Continental Congress in 1774 and again in 1776. The Continental Congress was no place for sympathizers to the Crown, and, again, several members of that body pressured Ross to declare his loyalty one way or the other.

Perhaps because of the outbreak of actual hostilities and the subversive conduct of the Crown, George Ross made it loud and clear that his loyalty was now with the colonies and their push for complete independence.

According to some reports, it was also about this time that Ross thought it might make sense for both General George Washington and Robert Morris to meet his step-niece, Betsy Ross. She had developed the earned reputation for being the best seamstress in the area and might be the perfect person to help with the design of the first flag for the new nation.

Well, in May 1776, General George Washington, Robert Morris, and George Ross—the uncle of her late husband, John—did indeed walk into Betsy's home.

As it turned out, **Betsy Ross**—born Elizabeth Griscom on **January 1, 1752**—and **George Washington** attended the same church, with the general and his wife, Martha, sitting in the pew right next to her. For that reason and more, the meeting was quite comfortable. According to **Betsy**, the general showed her a rough design for the flag, and she went right to work.

It should be noted that before she helped to design and sew the flag, she had already lost her first husband to the Revolution. She would lose her second husband to the war as well. On top of those tragedies, the British redcoats forcefully appropriated her home to house their soldiers.

Betsy Ross was a remarkable woman and an exceptional Patriot. **George Ross** knew that and took great pride in introducing the commander of the Continental Army and the financer of the Revolution to his highly accomplished and sophisticated step-niece.

The year **1776** proved to be very busy for **George Ross**. At the same time, he was serving in the Continental Congress, serving as a provincial legislator, serving as a colonel in the Continental Army, and negotiating a treaty with the Northwestern Indians on behalf of his colony. All the while, he still found the time to sign the **Declaration of Independence**.

In **1777** he was reelected to the Continental Congress but ended up resigning his seat due to his deteriorating health. In March **1778**, he achieved his last political and professional hurrah by being appointed to a judgeship in the Pennsylvania Court of Admiralty.

George Ross passed away in that office in July **1779**. He was forty-nine years of age.

CHAPTER THIRTY-NINE

Caesar Rodney

Would you ride for fourteen hours straight on multiple horses through darkness and vicious thunderstorms to potentially save the **Declaration of Independence?**

Caesar Rodney did that and so much more.

Rodney was born in **1728** on his family's 800-acre estate just outside of Dover, Delaware. Whatever education he received was given to him by his father and mother at home.

Right around **Rodney's** seventeenth birthday, his father passed away, leaving the estate in his young hands. He took the responsibility quite seriously and for the next decade or so, managed and grew the estate while looking after his mother and siblings.

In **1755**, he was commissioned as the high sheriff of Kent County, Delaware, under the command of the royal government. Not only did he excel in that position, but he proceeded to add titles to his name and work history. In, around, and after that time, **Rodney** was also a justice of the Superior Court, the registrar of wills, the recorder of deeds, the clerk of the orphan's court, and a justice of the peace.

During that decade or so, he did not give colonial or international politics or intrigue much thought. He was content to live his life under the supervision and occasional edicts of the Crown.

What changed that mindset to turn him into a Patriot advocating for complete independence from England? The Stamp Act.

As was reported several decades later:

> When the Stamp Act excited the jealousy and alarm of the Colonies, Mr. Rodney boldly proclaimed his sentiments in opposition to it and several antecedent acts of injustice which the British government had inflicted upon her Colonies in America.[36]

From 1761 to 1776, Rodney was a member of the Delaware colonial legislature. Additionally, and much more importantly, in 1774 he had been elected to the Continental Congress and reelected in 1776.

During that time, Rodney was also appointed as a brigadier general for the militia, a title and a responsibility he took quite seriously. So seriously in fact that he was often away from the Continental Congress and Philadelphia tending to military matters back home in Delaware.

And it was because of those duties and his being away from Philadelphia that things really got interesting. On the night of July 1, 1776, Rodney received an urgent message from fellow Delaware member Thomas McKean informing him that their friend and fellow Delaware member George Read had signaled he was going to vote against independence for the colonies. Because of that, McKean pleaded with **Rodney** to head back to Philadelphia immediately to break the one-one tie between him and **Read** so Delaware could officially vote for independence.

As soon as he got the message, General **Rodney** jumped on his horse—and then several others—and made the eighty-mile trip to Philadelphia, through multiple thunderstorms and darkness in less than fourteen hours to cast the deciding vote for Delaware on **July 2, 1776**.

After the vote, he returned back home to Delaware to reassume command of the militia, a command he served with great distinction in a number of battles.

In **1778**, **Rodney** was elected president (governor) of Delaware and served for three years.

Sadly, from at least his late teens, **Rodney** had suffered from a growth on his face that continually got worse. As it did, he tried to hide it beneath a face covering so as not to draw the attention or cruel remarks of people around him. Without a doubt, that growth—and the negative attention it brought him—was one of the main reasons he never married.

Rodney was elected to the national Congress in **1782** but declined the honor as he felt the growth was now winning the battle over his body and health and his time to leave this Earth would soon be upon him.

Caesar Rodney passed away on the grounds of his estate in Dover, Delaware, in **1784** at fifty-five years of age.

CHAPTER FORTY

George Read

How can one be the *only* signer to vote *against* independence during the final Continental Congress tally on 𝔍𝔲𝔩𝔶 𝟤, 1776, and still get to sign the 𝔇𝔢𝔠𝔩𝔞𝔯𝔞𝔱𝔦𝔬𝔫 𝔬𝔣 𝔍𝔫𝔡𝔢𝔭𝔢𝔫𝔡𝔢𝔫𝔠𝔢 one month later?

Worse than that—at least for 𝔠𝔞𝔢𝔰𝔞𝔯 𝔯𝔬𝔡𝔫𝔢𝔶—it was because of that "no" vote that 𝔯𝔬𝔡𝔫𝔢𝔶 had to ride for fourteen hours through the darkness and thunderstorms in the first place, as described above.

𝔊𝔢𝔬𝔯𝔤𝔢 𝔯𝔢𝔞𝔡 was born in Cecil County, Maryland, in 1733. While 𝔊𝔢𝔬𝔯𝔤𝔢 was still an infant, his wealthy father relocated the family to New Castle, Delaware.

As a young boy, his father sent him to school in Pennsylvania and then on to Philadelphia to study law under the supervision of a very successful attorney. 𝔯𝔢𝔞𝔡 was admitted to the bar in 1753 and then returned to New Castle to practice law.

For the next decade, he grew his business along with his wealth. As he was doing so, he began to pay more and more attention to the issues cropping up between the colonies and the Crown. By nature, 𝔯𝔢𝔞𝔡 was cautious and quite moderate in his thinking. Some of the heated rhetoric between both sides was truly beginning to alarm him.

In 1763, his life took two important turns. First, he met, fell in love with, and married Gertrude Ross Till, a woman, who as it turned out, was the sister of future co-signer of the Declaration, George Ross of Pennsylvania.

The second thing of importance that happened to Read that year was that he was made the Crown's attorney general for Delaware. He held this position until 1774, and it helped to create the ambivalence in his mind regarding taking sides between England and the colonies.

But that ambivalence began to wane because of two punitive measures enacted by the Crown. The first, of course, was the Stamp Act. Even more deeply troubling to Read was the Boston Port Bill, the petty and highly punishing measure launched by the British Parliament against the people of Boston as reprisal for the Boston Tea Party.

As was reported coming up on two centuries ago:

> On the thirty-first of March, 1774, the British Parliament passed an act for the punishment of the people of Boston for the destruction of tea in the harbor, on the sixteenth of December previous. It provided for the virtual and actual closing of the port…. Thus all business was suddenly crushed in Boston, and the inhabitants were reduced to great misery, overawed as they were by large bodies of armed troops. The people of the Colonies deeply sympathized with them, and lent them generous aid.[37]

One of those people was **George Read**. Not only did he raise a great deal of money from friends, neighbors, and colleagues for the literally starving men, women, and children of Boston, but he also donated generously from his own funds as well.

While this atrocity against the people of Boston pushed his heart and mind more toward total independence for the colonies, it was still not the tipping point.

Even though he was elected to the Continental Congress in 1774, his mind was still open to hearing both sides, and he could not pick the one to which he would pledge his life, his fortune, and his future.

That continual fence-straddling—and increased angering of his fellow members in the Continental Congress—brings us back to **July 1, 1776**, when he let it be known to his fellow Delaware delegate **Thomas McKean** that he was not going to vote for independence. It was at that point that the horrified and outraged McKean sent for **Caesar Rodney**.

All that truly curious conduct by **Read** raises the question: "Why did he act in such a wishy-washy—or cowardly as some members believed—manner?"

One theory that would make immediate sense is that because **Read**—with his beloved family—lived and worked in an area still highly loyal to the Crown, he had literally received death threats against himself and his family if he voted for independence.

Whatever the real reason he voted no initially, once independence from the Crown was declared, **Read** screwed up the appropriate amount of courage needed to sign the **Declaration of Independence**.

While he may have partially shamed himself with regard to the **Declaration** and did create some literal late-night intrigue and angst with **Rodney**'s own midnight ride, **Read** more than made up for it in **1787** during the Constitutional Convention in Philadelphia.

Not only did he deeply believe in the Constitution, but he also became one of the leading spokesman advocating for the rights of the smaller states. As it turned out, Read was so passionate about the Constitution that he energized the rest of the Delaware delegation to enthusiastically vote for its approval.

Thanks in large measure to the efforts by **George Read**, Delaware became our first state on **December 7, 1787**.

From **1789** to **1793**, Read served in the US Senate until he resigned to become the chief justice of the Delaware Supreme Court, a position he still held when he passed away in **1798** at sixty-five years of age.

CHAPTER FORTY-ONE

Thomas McKean

𝕿he legacy and legend of 𝕿𝕙𝖔𝖒𝖆𝖘 𝕸𝖈𝕶𝖊𝖆𝖓 includes two important milestones: he was the *very last* delegate to actually sign the 𝕯𝖊𝖈𝖑𝖆𝖗𝖆𝖙𝖎𝖔𝖓 𝖔𝖋 𝕴𝖓𝖉𝖊𝖕𝖊𝖓𝖉𝖊𝖓𝖈𝖊, and he was so beloved by the people of Delaware and Pennsylvania that both wanted to claim him as their own. Quite amazingly, New Jersey could have also insisted he was one of theirs.

𝕸𝖈𝕶𝖊𝖆𝖓 was born in New London, Pennsylvania, on 𝕸𝖆𝖗𝖈𝖍 19, 1734. His father was both a farmer and a tavern keeper, but young 𝕿𝖍𝖔𝖒𝖆𝖘 became interested in the study of law. By the age of twenty-one, he not only proved himself to be a bit of a prodigy when it came to the law, but he also actually got himself admitted to the bar in both Pennsylvania and Delaware. That accomplishment heralded the beginning of one of the greatest work résumés ever known to the colonies.

If we look at just the positions he held in Delaware, we see that he was a sheriff, militia captain, trustee of a loan office, customs collector, deputy attorney general, and member of the legislature, where he served as the speaker of the lower house.

In 1774, he was elected to the Continental Congress as a delegate from Delaware. Two years later, on **July 1, 1776**, he dispatched the urgent message to **Caesar Rodney** to return to Philadelphia immediately as he had just learned that **George Read** was going to vote against independence.

Except for about a one-year period starting at the very end of 1776, **McKean** remained an active member of the Continental Congress until 1783. So active, in fact, that for a brief period in 1781, he served as its president.

Around that time, **McKean** was commissioned as a colonel in the New Jersey Militia, where he was almost killed in action while leading troops as British cannon balls fell all about him. In fact, it was **McKean**'s valiant service in New Jersey that caused him to miss signing the **Declaration of Independence** with the majority of other delegates in August 1776. Because he was off fighting the redcoats, he did not get around to signing the document until sometime after **January 18, 1777**. Again, making him the *very last* delegate to sign.

One would naturally think that all of the travel, the multiple jobs, and the up-close-and personal horrors of war would have been enough for **McKean** to call it a day and retire to the countryside in peace. Not that guy.

In 1777, he was appointed the chief justice of Pennsylvania. He somehow held this office for almost two decades while simultaneously serving the people of Delaware. And just what was he doing for the people of Delaware during that same time? Only serving as the president (governor) of the colony.

At some point, the leaders of Pennsylvania, Delaware, and New Jersey had to believe that there was more than one **Thomas McKean**. Maybe he was the first clone known to humanity, all of them looking, talking, and serving in the exact same manner. They had to think that way because it was simply impossible that one man could do so many jobs in so many towns, counties, colonies, and then states all at the same time.

Impossible.

Except he did it…and had no intention of stopping.

In 1787, he was part of the Constitutional Convention.

Surely, that was enough.

Nope. In 1799, he was elected governor of Pennsylvania. And when some of his political enemies tried to have him impeached—maybe they were just truly sick of seeing his face everywhere they went—they failed miserably, and he was elected twice more by the people before retiring on his own terms in 1812.

𝔗homas 𝔐c𝔎ean—the Revolutionary résumé ruler—passed away on 𝔍une 24, 1817, at eighty-three years of age.

Chapter Forty-Two

William Floyd

Once again, we have a signer who was born into great wealth but orphaned at a fairly early age.

William Floyd was born on his family's estate on Long Island on December 17, 1734. As his family had immigrated to America and the New York area from Wales about eight decades before, its wealth, land ownings, and power were well established by the time young William came along.

He was being educated at home by his parents and various tutors when tragedy struck. His mother and father were both taken from him weeks apart, and he was left to his own devices in his midteens.

Thanks to the examples set by his mother and father, as well as the home education they provided, William was mature beyond his years and rather easily settled into running the large estate and massive amount of property left to him.

William wanted for nothing and did not seem to be in a rush to do anything other than tend his holdings, fish from time to time, and host various friends for weekend parties.

That lifestyle quickly changed in his midtwenties when he met and then married Hannah Jones.

Like many New Yorkers in the 1760s, Floyd was not particularly concerned with what was happening between the colonies and the Crown at that time. Life was good. Life was simple. And he saw no reason to rock the boat. But as Floyd was about to quickly learn, sometimes others not only want to rock that boat as violently as possible but also rob and even kill all within it.

Toward the very end of that decade, Floyd became an official of the Brookhaven area, where his estate was located. Slowly but surely, he began to spout off about the unfair taxes and treatment being levied against the colonists by the Crown. As he did so, his voice began to reach more and more of the ears of his neighbors.

Because of that, Floyd was elected to represent New York in the First Continental Congress in 1774. Being neither a lawyer nor really a politician, Floyd chose slow and easy as his course of action while attending that first congress. He spoke with as many delegates as possible, took notes during the meetings, and tried to bring himself up to the continually accelerating speed of almost all in that congress.

The face of war had appeared over the horizon, and Floyd knew he had a responsibility to his family and friends back home to be as educated and prepared as possible.

By 1776, he was caught up and then some.

After signing the Declaration of Independence on August 2, 1776, Floyd went back home to fight for his new nation. He did so by leading a militia unit in his Long Island area, engaging in battle with the redcoats on several occasions.

Soon thereafter, the American forces were overwhelmed, and **Floyd** was barely able to evacuate his wife and children to Connecticut in time. They were forced into exile for seven long years. Quite tragically, **Floyd** never saw his wife again as she died in 1781.

Soon after he got his family to safety, **Floyd**'s estate was overrun by the British, his sheep and cattle slaughtered, and most of what he owned destroyed.

Upon returning to his then-ransacked estate and property in 1783, with his now motherless children in tow, **Floyd** decided the only course of action was to rebuild what he had lost and try to start his life anew.

He did so in a quite spectacular manner. Not only did he rebuild his property, but he also remarried and reentered public service. In 1789 **Floyd** was elected to the first United States Congress under the new Constitution, where he served for two years.

Then speaking of "eccentric," in 1803 at almost seventy years of age, **Floyd** decided that he wanted to move to a very remote area in upstate New York where he had purchased a large parcel of land years earlier. His children were naturally shocked by the decision and tried to talk him out of it.

Floyd would have none of it. His mind was made up. For some reason only he knew, he wanted to spend the remainder of his life basically alone with nature. That determined, he turned over his massive Long Island estate to his son and never looked back.

Amazingly, he lived another seventeen-plus years in that remote area, which brought him so much peace of mind. **William Floyd** passed in 1821 at eighty-six years of age.

Chapter Forty-Three

Philip Livingston

For most of us, it would not be too difficult to understand why an ultrawealthy, seemingly patrician snob who was initially not too keen on independence and looked down his nose at the "unwashed masses" who made up the 𝔖𝔬𝔫𝔰 𝔬𝔣 𝔏𝔦𝔟𝔢𝔯𝔱𝔶 might have been seen as a bit of a problem by some of his fellow colonists seeking to free their throats from the unrelenting pressure exerted on them by the dung-covered boot of the Crown.

𝔓𝔥𝔦𝔩𝔦𝔭 𝔏𝔦𝔳𝔦𝔫𝔤𝔰𝔱𝔬𝔫 was born in Albany, New York, on 𝔍𝔞𝔫𝔲𝔞𝔯𝔶 15, 1716, into a—drumroll please—very wealthy family. How wealthy? Well, his family home also had a name; it was called Livingston Manor. The estate itself stretched over 160,000 acres.

You read that correctly. The 𝔏𝔦𝔳𝔦𝔫𝔤𝔰𝔱𝔬𝔫 estate equated to about 250 square miles of property. Or the equivalent of a small European country.

Pampered young 𝔓𝔥𝔦𝔩𝔦𝔭 was tutored at home before being sent off to Yale College to finish his education. After graduating in 1737, he returned to Albany to apprentice with his father in the mercantile business before entering the import business in New York City.

Approximately three years later, he married a young woman by the name of Christina Ten Broeck, the wealthy daughter of—wait for it—the mayor of Albany.

What is that F. Scott Fitzgerald line again about the rich?

Soon, between family money and what he was bringing in on his own, Livingston built three new homes for himself and his wife and growing family: a stone townhouse in Manhattan, a forty-acre estate in Brooklyn Heights, and another home in Kingston, New York.

By 1754—after donating a great deal of money to institutions he was directly interested in, such as the New York Society Library, the New York Chamber of Commerce, and New York Hospital—he entered politics after being appointed as an alderman of the East Ward of New York City. In 1759 he made the jump to elected representative to the Provincial Assembly of New York City, which was still loyal to the Crown.

At this point, it once again makes sense to remember that the vast majority of the wealthy people in the colonies sided with the oppressive Crown. No family was wealthier than the "lord of the manor" at the Livingston Manor.

While Philip made it known that he did not exactly approve of the taxes imposed on the colonists by the Crown, he also proclaimed that he greatly disapproved of the civil disobedience of the Sons of Liberty and the rabble that made up its numbers.

Okay.

None of that is a surprise when one realizes that Livingston also supported the "Olive Branch Petition." A sniveling—at least in the minds of such delegates as John Adams—attempt at "reconciliation" between the colonies and the Crown was sent directly to King George III, with the hope that the "kindly king" would somehow save the colonies from the mean and despicable Parliament.

That "Olive Branch" was humiliatingly snapped in two by a king who refused to even read it. That insult from the king only served to harden the resolve of the colonists against the Crown and, in fact, hasten the war.

In some very real ways, the Livingston family was the colonial American version of the Rockefeller family. What you could not get appointed to, you could sometimes buy.

By 1774 not only was Philip Livingston made part of the Continental Congress, but his brother William and first-cousin-once-removed Robert also would join him in that august body. Robert most ably did so while serving on the Committee of Five entrusted with drafting the Declaration of Independence.

While Philip Livingston may have had what seemed like all the money in the world at that time, his wealth did not impress the British Army invading New York City. They seized both his home in Manhattan and his estate in Brooklyn Heights.

Because of that, Livingston fled with his family to his multiacre estate in Kingston. Later, the British would burn to the ground the town of Kingston along with the mansion of his first cousin, Robert R. Livingston, which lay just across the Hudson River.

While attending the Continental Congress in 1778, Philip Livingston suddenly and unexpectedly passed away where he stood. He was sixty-two years of age.

CHAPTER FORTY-FOUR

Francis Lewis

peaking of the 𝕾𝖔𝖓𝖘 𝖔𝖋 𝕷𝖎𝖇𝖊𝖗𝖙𝖞, next we come to another New Yorker who not only did not look down his nose at it and the rabble of which that Patriotic organization was composed, but very well may have led a wing of it for his colony.

𝔉𝔯𝔞𝔫𝔠𝔦𝔰 𝔏𝔢𝔴𝔦𝔰 was born in Wales in 1713. He was—a tragic recurring theme among the signers—orphaned when he was but four years of age. Fortunately for him, relatives in London were able to take him in, treat him as one of their own children, and give him a good education at the Westminster School.

Upon graduation, he became an apprentice at a very successful mercantile house in London. Not only was he a dedicated employee, but he also endeavored to learn every facet of the business. He did so because he had decided he wanted to open his own mercantile shop—but not in London. He wanted to move to America and the great promise he was told it held for a young man with his work ethic and ambition.

Soon after his twenty-first birthday, 𝕷𝖊𝖂𝖎𝖘 felt he had enough experience—and money put away—to sail to America and start his new life. Upon his arrival in New York City, he set up a partnership with a friend. After doing so, he bounced back and forth between New York City and Philadelphia for over a year before picking New York as his permanent home.

Good thing he did. Because also in New York was the sister of his partner and his future wife, Elizabeth Annesley. Francis and Elizabeth had three children who lived into adulthood.

Not only did Francis prove to be an exceptional business-man, but he truly loved to travel and see the world and would often accompany his goods as they set off to ports in Europe, Russia, and even the African continent.

In 1756, the life of Francis Lewis changed in a very dramatic and damaging way. It was then, while working as a clothing supplier for the British Army during the French and Indian War, that he was taken prisoner by the French after most of the British soldiers around him had been slain. At first, he was taken to a prisoner of war camp in Canada run by the French. Soon thereafter, he was transported to France, where in total he was held prisoner for seven long years.

Amazingly, upon his release, Francis headed right back to New York City with the same positive attitude that had carried him through life to that point.

After rebuilding his business and much of his fortune, Francis decided to retire and move from New York City to Long Island. The year was 1765.

You got it. That same year, the British Parliament imposed that punitive Stamp Act upon the colonists, an act that truly angered Lewis.

He loved his new country and knew how many of his friends and neighbors were struggling simply to survive. Because of that, he felt this new tax upon them would be devastating. And because of that, he slowly but surely inserted himself into the Patriot cause.

Not to long after that, there were rumors that the New York contingent of the 𝔖𝔬𝔫𝔰 𝔬𝔣 𝔏𝔦𝔟𝔢𝔯𝔱𝔶 was being headed up by none other than...𝔉𝔯𝔞𝔫𝔠𝔦𝔰 𝔏𝔢𝔴𝔦𝔰.

Because of his growing voice—and possible nighttime civil disobedience activities—in 1775, he was elected to the Continental Congress. As one who knew a great deal about shipping, he volunteered to help with the committee seeking to build the Continental Navy.

Just about three months later, he proudly signed the 𝔇𝔢𝔠𝔩𝔞𝔯𝔞𝔱𝔦𝔬𝔫 𝔬𝔣 𝔍𝔫𝔡𝔢𝔭𝔢𝔫𝔡𝔢𝔫𝔠𝔢.

But, as mentioned, the Crown targeted those who signed the 𝔇𝔢𝔠𝔩𝔞𝔯𝔞𝔱𝔦𝔬𝔫 for as much retribution as possible. And because of that, Francis paid a terrible price.

By the fall of 1776, the British Army had already seized New York City. Soon thereafter, they approached the Long Island home of 𝔏𝔢𝔴𝔦𝔰 and destroyed it and all his worldly possessions. Much worse than that, they took his beloved Elizabeth as a prisoner and held her for months as a punishment to him for daring to sign the 𝔇𝔢𝔠𝔩𝔞𝔯𝔞𝔱𝔦𝔬𝔫. While they held her, her British jailers treated her in the most barbaric of ways.

When she was finally released by the British, she was already all but gone from this Earth. When she passed as the result of her brutal treatment, 𝔉𝔯𝔞𝔫𝔠𝔦𝔰 became grief-stricken beyond repair.

Soon after she died, 𝔉𝔯𝔞𝔫𝔠𝔦𝔰 𝔏𝔢𝔴𝔦𝔰 retired from the Continental Congress and moved back to New York City to be with his sons and their families until he finally passed in 1802 at eighty-nine years of age.

Chapter Forty-Five

Lewis Morris

From one "Lewis" we roll right into the next. Only this one—like 𝔓hilip 𝔏ivingston—represented the upper crust of the upper crust of New York. That comparison aside, this incredibly rich guy did all in his power to help crush the Crown, and when it became his turn to sign the 𝔇eclaration of 𝔍ndependence—and his own "death warrant"—he loudly proclaimed to those gathered with him: "*Damn the consequences. Give me the pen.*"[38]

𝔏ewis 𝔐orris was born on his family's massive estate in New York—named Morrisania—in 1726. Also tutored at home, when he was of age, he was sent off to Yale College, graduating in 1746. Upon his graduation, he returned home to take over the day-to-day running of his family's massive estate.

Just about two years later, he married a very wealthy young woman by the name of Mary Walton. 𝔏ewis and Mary would go on to have ten children.

When his father passed away in 1762, 𝔏ewis was officially in charge of all. Soon after that, people began to notice a change in 𝔐orris. While he was elected to what was then the royal government's New York Assembly, he began to voice louder and increasingly less polite criticisms of the Crown, most especially with regard to the Stamp Act and the royal governor's order that the assembly provide funds for the British troops being housed in New York.

Once again, a strong voice against the Crown was noticed, and Morris was elected to the Second Continental Congress in 1776. Because of his owning Morrisania and other land and property, Morris knew he had more to lose than other wealthy colonists. But even at that, he refused to bite his tongue and take the easy way out as so many of his wealthy contemporaries were doing. If anything, his voice kept getting louder with each Crown overreach and atrocity he witnessed.

As part of the Continental Congress, Morris served on the committees tasked with arming the troops and with Indian affairs. On July 2, 1776, Morris was greatly offended to know that every colony but New York would be voting for the Declaration of Independence. One week later, he made it a personal point of honor to return to Philadelphia to sign what he considered to be the greatest document ever introduced to humanity.

By 1777, he was back in New York serving in the legislature and as a judge.

But, once again, there would be a high price to pay for those Founding Fathers who dared to sign the Declaration. As was reported coming up on two hundred years ago with regard to Lewis Morris:

> He plainly foresaw what actually happened—
> his home ruined, his farm wasted, his forest of
> a thousand acres despoiled, his cattle carried

off, and his family driven into exile by the
invading foe.[39]

While Morrisania was leveled by the British, **Morris** was
beyond proud to know that three of his sons went on to serve
in the Continental Army in the fight against the Crown.

Upon the completion of the war, **Morris** put all of his energy into rebuilding his home and his lands. As he was doing
that, 1784 saw him serving on the first Board of Regents of
the University of New York and in 1788 he became one of
the leading voices in support of Alexander Hamilton's bid for
ratification of the United States Constitution.

Lewis Morris passed away at his beloved Morrisania in
1798 at seventy-one years of age.

CHAPTER FORTY-SIX

Richard Stockton

People tend to forget that, before and during the Revolutionary War, the eyes and the ears of those Americans still loyal to the brutal Crown were *everywhere.*

Richard Stockton found that out the hard way when, as the British Army was closing in on his town, he fled with his wife and children to hide out with a friend. Unfortunately for him, some of the Loyalists in the area realized what he had done and revealed his location to the redcoats for reward money. He was captured and brutalized by the British while in prison.

Stockton was born near Princeton, New Jersey, on **October 1, 1730.** As the son of a wealthy landowner and judge, young Stockton also wanted for nothing as he pursued his education. His education eventually took place at the College of New Jersey, which later morphed into Princeton University—*a now alleged institution of higher learning where much of the faculty and student body hate the* **Founding Fathers** *and are doing all in their power to eradicate them.*

After graduating in **1748, Stockton** decided to pursue a career in law and went on to become one of the most successful and prominent lawyers in all of the colonies. In 1755, he married Annis Boudinot, with whom he would go on to have six children.

For the next decade after that, Stockton, built up his practice, increased his—by then—already considerable wealth, and lived a life of extreme comfort and culture.

But then came 1765. Just about the same time the Stamp Act was being foisted upon the colonies, Stockton became part of the Royal Council of New Jersey. At first, his was a voice of moderation arguing that the colonies should be represented in the British Parliament. But as the backlash against the Stamp Act grew, so did Stockton's beliefs that the Crown was treating the colonies in an unfair and even demeaning manner.

In 1774, Stockton was appointed as a justice of the Supreme Court of New Jersey. Two years later, as some of the New Jersey delegates to the Continental Congress were opposing independence for the colonies, New Jersey quickly elected Stockton and John Witherspoon to replace two of them. Both men then joined the rest of the delegation in signing the Declaration of Independence.

One of the committees Stockton was assigned to was entrusted with monitoring the war effort. As such, he was sent on a fact-finding mission to evaluate the Northern Department of the Continental Army. What he observed horrified and saddened him. Most of the men had no shoes and were going barefoot.

Said Stockton at the time:

> There is not a single shoe or stocking to be
> had in this part of the world, or I would ride

a hundred miles through the woods and purchase then with my own money.[40]

Unfortunately, as alluded to above, Stockton would soon
have no money or possessions of his own. After he was taken
prisoner, his British captors intentionally starved and tortured
him because he signed the Declaration—an abuse that went on
every single day for over five weeks.

When he was finally released, he returned to Princeton to
learn that British General Cornwallis himself had occupied
his home while he was being tortured in prison. More than
that, upon his return, he found all his household belong-
ings destroyed, his crops burned to the ground, his livestock
slaughtered. And even more upsetting to him, his personal
library of over one thousand books had been burned by the
British Army as they fled the area.

Beaten, battered, and mentally broken, one of formerly
richest men in New Jersey now found himself penniless and
living in poverty. As his health continued to slip away because
of the abuse he suffered in a British prison, he tried to reopen
his law practice to bring in any income.

Quite humiliating for him, as he was attempting to do
that, he had to resort to begging his family and friends for the
money needed simply to survive.

Never free of pain or suffering again, Richard Stockton
passed away on February 28, 1781, at fifty years of age.

CHAPTER FORTY-SEVEN

John Witherspoon

Speaking of Princeton University, we come to a man who not only put that institution on the academic and world map but also led it magnificently for over a quarter of a century.

That, of course, was *then*.

Today, hundreds of pampered, tenured, and liberal faculty members want his statue and any mention of him removed from the campus forever. Faculty who have no problem bringing about a "dark age" much more dangerous than the first. Why *more dangerous*? Again, for the simple reason that the Left and Far Left control the media, academia, science, medicine, and entertainment…

…a groupthink 𝕵𝕠𝕙𝕟 𝕎𝕚𝕥𝕙𝕖𝕣𝕤𝕡𝕠𝕠𝕟 would have condemned with all of his might until his very last breath.

𝕵𝕠𝕙𝕟 𝕎𝕚𝕥𝕙𝕖𝕣𝕤𝕡𝕠𝕠𝕟 was born in Scotland just outside of Edinburgh on 𝕱𝖊𝖇𝖗𝖚𝖆𝖗𝖞 5, 1722.

His father was a minister, and so he was destined to become one himself. Education was incredibly important in the 𝕎𝕚𝕥𝕙𝕖𝕣𝕤𝕡𝕠𝕠𝕟 household, and young John got the best possible. By the time he reached twenty years of age, he had received master's degrees in both divinity and the arts from the University of Edinburgh. Soon after that, he became one of Scotland's leading ministers.

Now, it was when young Witherspoon became the minister for Beith that things really got interesting for him—as in, locked in a dungeon interesting.

In January of 1746, the twenty-three-year-old minister heard that there was to be a battle between the army of King George II and the Scottish Highlanders loyal to Prince Charles Stuart (Bonnie Prince Charlie).

At this point, the history gets a little murky. A number of accounts record that Minister Witherspoon simply led a group of his parishioners to the outskirts of the area "from curiosity to see a battle."[41]

Others said he went there to fight on the side of the British and King George II (an act, one might assume to be highly unlikely for a man of God), and still others claim he was on the side of the Highlanders because of his growing animosity toward the Crown because of the numerous atrocities it had already committed in Scotland.

Whatever the true account, all seem to agree that because he was there, after the battle he was rounded up and imprisoned in the Doune Castle. One of the earliest mentions of that incident from almost two centuries ago recounts:

> While he was stationed at Beith, the battle of Falkirk took place, between the forces of George the Second, and Prince Charles Stuart, during the commotion known as the Scotch rebellion, in 1745–6. Mr. Witherspoon and others went to witness the battle, which

proved victorious to the rebels: and he, with several others, were taken prisoners, and for some time confined in the castle of Doune.

Now—and of at least interest to me and the Greater MacKinnon Clan originating from the Isle of Skye—we have a "six degrees of history" connection to that time. For it was then, that our great, great, great, great, great (math was never my strong suit in school) relative John MacKinnon literally saved the life of Bonnie Prince Charlie.

Naturally, you may have your doubts about this account and believe it to be made up. Okay, let's look at the back-label of a bottle of Drambuie—Prince Charles Edward's Liqueur.

On the back label of almost every single bottle ever produced over the now centuries, we have this:

> In 1745 when Bonnie Prince Charlie came to Scotland in his gallant attempt to regain the throne of his ancestors, he gave the recipe of his personal liqueur to a MacKinnon of Skye for saving his life...

From the Drambuie website itself, we have this:

> The story of Drambuie began in 1745 when it arrived on British shores under the guardianship of its original custodian, Prince Charles Edward Stuart (known as Bonnie Prince Charlie). It was the Prince's personal draft, and he drank a few drops each day for strength and vitality.

The Prince had travelled from Rome to raise
an army in the hopes of restoring his exiled
family, The House of Stuart to the throne
of Great Britain. His unfortunate enterprise
ended with defeat at the Battle of Culloden
in 1746. Pursued by the King's men he fled to
The Isle of Skye. After a period of exile on the
island his pursuers caught up with him and
his fate lay with the Clan MacKinnon who
bravely helped the Prince escape the British
Isles for good.

In thanks for his unwavering loyalty the
Prince gave John MacKinnon, the clan leader,
the secret recipe to his personal liqueur, a
gift that the Clan were to treasure down the
generations.[42]

All that to wonder if Minister John Witherspoon knew
of the connection between Bonnie Prince Charlie and the
MacKinnon Clan? As he was a highly educated and curious
man and this history did play out in real time in his very back-
yard, it's not far-fetched at all to believe that he did.

Okay. Now back to *his* actual history.

How did Minister Witherspoon happen to come to America?
As it turned out, several prominent Americans played a role,
including Declaration signers Benjamin Rush and Richard
Stockton. Both men had met him while traveling in Scotland
and became immediately impressed with not only his intellect
and ability to write but most especially his decency.

Once they learned that the College of New Jersey was in search of a leader, both men whole heartedly recommended Minister 𝔚𝔦𝔱𝔥𝔢𝔯𝔰𝔭𝔬𝔬𝔫. When first offered the position, Witherspoon most politely turned it down because his wife, Elizabeth, was understandably fearful of crossing the ocean on a ship. After a conversation with 𝔅𝔢𝔫𝔧𝔞𝔪𝔦𝔫 𝔕𝔲𝔰𝔥 alleviated her fears, she and her husband immigrated to New Jersey in 1768.

As the new president of the college, not only was he personally responsible for making it one of the most respected institutions of higher learning in the world, but in the process he also introduced his calm, reasoned, and faith-based voice to the people of America.

As the winds of Revolution and war blew across his happy and fruitful campus, Minister 𝔚𝔦𝔱𝔥𝔢𝔯𝔰𝔭𝔬𝔬𝔫 began to become more and more conflicted. As a man of God, he felt it best to abstain from any political concerns. But as a man who had witnessed the Crown abuse its power in the past, he came to believe that it would be irresponsible of him to ignore that same abuse now playing out in the colonies.

For that reason and more, he still somewhat hesitantly accepted appointment to the Committees for Correspondence and Safety in the first months of 1776. Later that year—in large part because of his exceptional work on those committees—he was elected to the Continental Congress.

Not only was 𝔚𝔦𝔱𝔥𝔢𝔯𝔰𝔭𝔬𝔬𝔫 impressed by the resolution so bravely put forth by 𝔕𝔦𝔠𝔥𝔞𝔯𝔡 𝔥𝔢𝔫𝔯𝔶 𝔏𝔢𝔢, but he also proudly voted for it and then on 𝔍𝔲𝔩𝔶 2, 1776, voted in favor of 𝔱𝔥𝔢 𝔇𝔢𝔠𝔩𝔞𝔯𝔞𝔱𝔦𝔬𝔫 𝔬𝔣 𝔍𝔫𝔡𝔢𝔭𝔢𝔫𝔡𝔢𝔫𝔠𝔢.

As those deliberations were taking place, 𝔚𝔦𝔱𝔥𝔢𝔯𝔰𝔭𝔬𝔬𝔫 heard another delegate in the room argue that the country was "not yet ripe for such a declaration." Minister Witherspoon then turned to that man and declared that the country "*was not only ripe for the measure, but in danger of rotting for the want of it.*"[43]

Witherspoon proved to be a very active member of the Continental Congress, serving on tens of committees while offering his opinion frequently to those around him.

In November of 1776, with the British Army advancing toward Princeton, he returned to shut down and then evacuate the College of New Jersey. He was right to do so.

The British forces not only destroyed most of the college but **Witherspoon**'s family home as well.

After the war, he dedicated the rest of his life to rebuilding the college. Sadly, soon thereafter, he suffered injuries to both eyes, which eventually cost him his sight.

Minister **John Witherspoon** passed away on his farm just outside Princeton in November 1794 at seventy-one years of age.

Chapter Forty-Eight

Francis Hopkinson

𝕯id he, or didn't he?

Unfortunately, while we will never be able to get a definitive answer, there is a fair of amount of anecdotal evidence pointing to the very real possibility that he did.

Did what?

Design the first American flag.

When most Americans—*of a certain age, as again they don't teach real American history anymore in our schools*—think of the American flag, the first name that pops up in their mind is the aforementioned 𝕭𝖊𝖙𝖘𝖞 𝕽𝖔𝖘𝖘. To be sure, Betsy was involved in that high-level meeting and did have some thoughts and suggestions.

Could two people have basically the same idea for a fairly unique design at about the exact same time? For sure. It happens all the time in the creative world.

Ultimately, whatever credit for designing the first American flag belongs to 𝕱𝖗𝖆𝖓𝖈𝖎𝖘 𝕳𝖔𝖕𝖐𝖎𝖓𝖘𝖔𝖓, the absolute fact of the matter is that he was one of the most creative people in the history of our nation and a true Renaissance man.

Hopkinson was born in 1737 in Philadelphia to a very wealthy and well-respected family. Both his mother and father were born and raised in England and had very close ties to the British aristocracy. Upon their arrival in Philadelphia, they settled in quite nicely with the blue bloods of that city.

Francis was the first of eight children born to the couple, so they made sure he had every advantage as a child. When his father passed away, fourteen-year-old Francis stepped up to help his mother with his siblings and navigate the uncertain waters of life.

Just about that same time, he enrolled in the College of Philadelphia. He focused on the study of law and was admitted to the bar soon after graduation.

But as it turned out, **Francis** was not that much interested in the law. Like many young people then and now, he was not quite sure which professional path he wanted to travel for the rest of his life. So instead of choosing right away, he decided to hop on a ship and head over to England to visit some family and get a bit more education, which included some study of the creative arts.

Upon his return to Philadelphia, he met and married a woman by the name of Ann Borden. Ann was not just any woman; she was the granddaughter of the man for whom her hometown of Bordentown, New Jersey, was named.

As **Francis** was kind of still searching for his identity at that time as he bounced about from being a lawyer to a failed shop owner to a poet, writer, and author, he had no trouble at all relocating his life to the town in New Jersey named after his new wife's family.

Once settled into Bordentown, **Francis** and Ann went on to have five children. Francis did start to get the hang of being a lawyer and was finally able to not only support his family but also put some money away as well.

That said, his mind always remained quite restless. As was said of him almost two centuries ago:

> Mr. Hopkinson was one of those modest, quiet men, on whom the mantle of true genius so frequently falls.[44]

Again, the shrinking number of American students who are taught honest American history today will know the name Thomas Paine. More importantly, they will know of the small book he published in January 1776 titled *Common Sense*.

Paine's revolutionary book during a Revolutionary time literally changed the history of that time. Not only was the book a scathing attack on the increasingly oppressive rule by the king and his Parliament, but it also offered up a well-thought-out solution to that tyranny: that the king's American subjects had a unique opportunity before them to *change the course of their own history* by creating their own nation, in which they would be free to govern themselves. At the darkest of times, Paine dared to promote American exceptionalism.

To say the book shook England and colonial America to its core would be an understatement. Once the colonists got their hands on it, they could not print the little book fast enough. By the end of the Revolutionary War, this "roadmap" to liberty had sold over 500,000 copies in a total population then of about 2.5 million people.

As a comparison, that would equate to an author selling about 70 million copies of a book in the United States today.

The importance of the book by **Thomas Paine** cannot be underestimated. Because a massive amount of the American population did read his suggested solutions to their misery, it ended up putting tremendous pressure on the **Founding Fathers** to find a way to declare and ultimately achieve independence.

All of that to say, that like **Francis Hopkinson**, **Paine** was a bit of a lost soul when it came to finding the proper path to walk in life. Until *Common Sense*, **Paine** had failed at about every job and endeavor he tried.

In some real ways, only his connection to **Benjamin Franklin** saved him. Mentally lost and broke at about thirty-seven years of age, **Paine** reached out to **Franklin**, whom he had met earlier in London. **Franklin** brought him to Philadelphia from London in 1774.

There—again, thanks to **Franklin**—he was able to find work as a lower-level journalist. But as he was doing so, both **Franklin** and **Benjamin Rush** realized that **Paine** had an incredible talent for writing and was, in fact, a natural storyteller. More than that, both men realized that **Paine**'s mind was capable of not only pinpointing the growing issues between the Crown and the colonies but also offering up workable solutions. For those reasons and more, they encouraged him to write the small book that would go on to impact the entire world.

Now, while the works of **Francis Hopkinson** never reached the massive success or readership of *Common Sense*, they did become fairly well-known, and they did inspire the colonists to further resist the tyranny of the Crown. Three of them became quite popular with the people: *A Pretty Story*, *The Battle of the Kegs*, and *The Prophecy*.

Because of his flair for words and his criticism of the Crown, in 1776 Hopkinson was elected to the Second Continental Congress. While there, the creative genius within him often took control.

As his fellow delegates would debate the issues of the day before him on the floor, Hopkinson would be sitting off to the side of the room drawing perfect caricatures of them in the sketch pad that almost never left his hands.

Throughout the Revolutionary War, this Renaissance man who wrote novels, music, operas, and painted—while later drafting the seal of the State of New Jersey and the seal of the Treasury—never stopped in his efforts to creatively make the case for American independence. He applied that same passion late in support of the United States Constitution.

All the while, he continued on with his then-prosperous legal career. In 1780, he was commissioned as a judge of the Admiralty. In 1790 he was appointed a federal circuit judge.

Sadly, all that creative genius stopped when, quite suddenly, Francis Hopkinson passed away while in Philadelphia in 1791 at fifty-three years of age.

CHAPTER FORTY-NINE

John Hart

aving the nickname "Honest John" attached to your life and reputation had to be both a blessing and a curse. No one is quite sure *how* John Hart got that moniker, as he was one of the few signers without a great deal of written history about his life.

It is believed that he was born somewhere between 1710 and 1714. Some of the earliest records of the time place his birth in Stonington, Connecticut, on the farm of his father, who soon relocated his family to another farm outside Hopewell, New Jersey.

In a bit of ironic history, some of the earliest records of the time also indicate that John Hart's father considered himself a very loyal subject of the king. So much so that about 1775, he helped to raise a volunteer force, which he named the "Jersey Blues" to fight at the side of British General Wolfe in Quebec. After surviving the battle in which Wolfe fell, the elder Hart returned to his farm in New Jersey and retired in some comfort, as he let his son John take over his duties.

With each passing day, young John Hart was gaining more and more of a reputation among his neighbors and friends for his unmatched work ethic, his passion to help anyone in need, and most especially his honesty. Hence, that nickname of "Honest John."

All was going quite well in his local and happy little life. He had married a wonderful woman by the name of Deborah Scudder, and they soon began to have enough children to fill several pews at their church.

But then—once again—came 1765 and that tipping point known as the Stamp Act. "Honest John" began to voice his strong disagreement with the act as well as his increasing anger at the Crown over their treatment of the people in Boston. And as he did, the people in the area who truly came to admire him for his integrity and passion began to pay attention.

Because of how he was viewed by his neighbors, he began to be elected or appointed to a variety of local offices, including justice of the peace, county judge, and member of the New Jersey Assembly. It was while he was serving in that body that he made it known to the royal governor and the people that he strongly opposed both parliamentary taxation upon the American people and the stationing of British troops within the colonies.

In large measure because of that, he was elected to the Second Continental Congress in 1776—and just in the nick of time.

Hart took his seat in that congress on July 1, 1776. The very next day, he voted for independence. And one month later on August 2, he signed the Declaration of Independence.

But, like so many other signers, he was made to pay a very high price for his "treason against the Crown." Just three months later when the British invaded New Jersey, they not only singled him out for retribution but also put a price on his head.

Hart arrived at his home just before the British Army only to find his beloved wife deathly ill and begging him to get their children into hiding before it was too late. Hart did so by placing the children with relatives and neighbors.

After doing so, he was forced to move from place to place in the increasingly frigid weather as the British attempted to hunt him down. As there was a price on his head, and hundreds of Loyalists in the area, Hart dared not stay for more than one night in any one location. As such, for the next number of frozen weeks, he hid in the woods and caves of the area, and his health took a terrible beating from the frigid conditions.

When he was finally able to return home after General George Washington and his troops had won the Battles of Princeton and Trenton, he found that his Deborah had died, his farm had been destroyed, his livestock slaughtered, and most of his trees and property burned to the ground by the cowardly retreating British redcoats.

After all of that, his health took a dramatic turn for the worse. In 1778 he was forced to retire from public life. And by 1779, John Hart passed away, at about sixty-eight years of age.

CHAPTER FIFTY

Abraham Clark

What price liberty and the birth of a new nation? For **Abraham Clark**, part of that price was having his two sons captured by the British Army, imprisoned, and tortured.

Clark was born on his family's small farm in New Jersey on **February 15, 1726**. He grew up as an only child in very humble means. Because of their dire financial situation, there was no time or especially money for education. **Clark**'s father needed him working the fields for hours every day so they could put food on their own table while hopefully being able to sell some of their yield for the money needed to purchase supplies.

In spite of that reality, **Abraham Clark** had a natural love for studying. He was most especially interested in the law and mathematics. So, between his never-ending and backbreaking chores, he self-educated himself as much as possible in those two subjects.

When he reached young adulthood, both he and his father realized that his thin, frail, and often sickly body was not built for a life of farming. But because he had taught himself quite a bit about mathematics, he was able to land a job as a surveyor.

By about his twenty-third birthday, **Abraham** met and married a young woman by the name of Sarah Hatfield. Together, the couple would have ten children.

As **Clark** was settling into his growing family life, he began to notice that more and more of his neighbors were having legal issues, which he believed his self-taught law education gave him enough knowledge and skill to solve. So that's what he began to do.

With more and more success, he began to reverse land disputes—often against wealthy landowners—in favor of his poor and humble neighbors. So much so, that **Clark** was soon known as the "poor man's counselor."

Unlike so many of the signers, **Clark** was far from wealthy and most likely would have been considered middle class or even lower middle class in his time. As such, he was not particularly fond of those from the upper classes who sought to take advantage of the poorer and less-educated colonists among them.

For that reason and more, his friends and neighbors came to believe that **Clark** would always have their back. And indeed, he did. Because of that belief, **Clark** soon served as the sheriff for Essex County, as well as in his local legislature. In 1776, he was elected to the Second Continental Congress and became one of the New Jersey delegates sent to the congress at the end of June. Within a span of but a few weeks, he voted for independence and then signed the **Declaration of Independence**.

Although he served in the Continental Congress for most of the Revolutionary War, much of his attention was focused on what was happening back in his home area of New Jersey. For he knew the British forces were all around it and it was only a matter of time before something terrible occurred.

That something turned out to be worse than terrible. Two of his sons were serving in the Continental Army, and both were captured by the British. When the British officers found out they were the boys of a "traitor" who had signed the **Declaration**, they were transferred to the infamous prison ship *Jersey*. It was infamous because of the American soldiers and colonists tortured and killed on that ship by their brutal and twisted captors.

After the war finally ended, **Abraham Clark** resumed his public service career by going back to the state legislature. In 1787 he also made it back to the Continental Congress.

After the adoption of the United States Constitution—which Clark initially opposed because it lacked a **Bill of Rights**—he served in the United States Congress from 1791 until he passed away in 1794. **Abraham Clark**—a true man of the people and *from the people*—was sixty-eight years of age at his death.

CHAPTER FIFTY-ONE

Josiah Bartlett

𝕬 s the vast majority of us know and have experienced, life is often not fair.

With that truism in mind, imagine being the *very first* Founding Father to vote for the 𝖉𝖊𝖈𝖑𝖆𝖗𝖆𝖙𝖎𝖔𝖓 𝖔𝖋 𝕴𝖓𝖉𝖊𝖕𝖊𝖓𝖉𝖊𝖓𝖈𝖊 and the *second* to sign it—after that 𝕵𝖔𝖍𝖓 𝕳𝖆𝖓𝖈𝖔𝖈𝖐 guy—and virtually no American knows your name.

There had to be a better-than-even chance that 𝕵𝖔𝖘𝖎𝖆𝖍 𝕭𝖆𝖗𝖙𝖑𝖊𝖙𝖙 was suffering from some form of signature envy after witnessing the work of art Hancock slapped onto the document to record his larger-than-life name.

𝕭𝖆𝖗𝖙𝖑𝖊𝖙𝖙 was born in Amesbury, Massachusetts, in November 1729 upon a fairly large farm owned by his family. While not wealthy, his family was comfortable. 𝕵𝖔𝖘𝖎𝖆𝖍 attended the local school as often as possible when not working the farm. In his midteens, he decided that he wanted to become a doctor and began it apprentice with a respected doctor in the Amesbury area. After about five years of helping the doctor with the basics in his medical practice, his master declared him qualified.

Suddenly, Josiah's titles went from farmhand and medical apprentice to Dr. Bartlett. Then, at about twenty-one years of age, Josiah was told of an urgent need for a doctor in the Kingston area of New Hampshire. As it was only about ten miles from his home in Massachusetts, Josiah felt it the perfect opportunity to start his career while still being close to his family.

After several years of establishing himself as a highly respected doctor, he ended up marrying a woman by the name of Mary Bartlett, who was part of the larger Bartlett family. The couple would go on to have over ten children.

Along with medicine, Dr. Bartlett had also developed a growing interest in all things political. As such, he became of a member of the colonial legislature. What immediately set him apart from other members was his resolve to push back against the royal governor when it came to issues involving British oppression of the colonies.

Because of that reputation, Bartlett was elected to the First Continental Congress. He unfortunately had to turn down that honor. As to why, some records indicate that as he was siding more and more with the colonies against the Crown, a number of his Loyalist neighbors were becoming infuriated with his behavior and decided to demonstrate that displeasure by...burning down his home.

No matter the reason, when he was elected to the Second Continental Congress, he readily accepted. Because he did, on July 2, 1776—because the northernmost colony of New Hampshire often voted first in the Continental Congress proceedings—he became the *very first* of The 56 to *vote* for independence, and as mentioned, one month later, became the *second* delegate to sign the Declaration of Independence.

After that momentous occasion, he mostly concentrated on the welfare of New Hampshire. That said, he did take the time to offer his strong backing to the US Constitution in 1787.

In 1790 Dr. Bartlett was elected governor of the State of New Hampshire, a position he held for four successful years.

In 1791 he helped to found the New Hampshire Medical Society and served as its very first president. Dr. Bartlett passed away in 1795 at sixty-five years of age.

CHAPTER FIFTY-TWO

William Whipple

At least in his late teens and early twenties, 𝔚𝔦𝔩𝔩𝔦𝔞𝔪 𝔚𝔥𝔦𝔭𝔭𝔩𝔢 was the American version of 𝔍𝔬𝔥𝔫 𝔓𝔞𝔲𝔩 𝔍𝔬𝔫𝔢𝔰. Minus running a mutineer through with a sword and getting to cuddle with Catherine the Great.

𝔚𝔦𝔩𝔩𝔦𝔞𝔪 𝔚𝔥𝔦𝔭𝔭𝔩𝔢 was born in what became Kittery, Maine, in 1730. By his early teens, he had become fascinated by the sea. By his midteens, he set off to sea to make his fortune and see the world.

As it turned out, he was exceptionally good at the sea life, and by the time he was twenty-one years of age, he had been made a master (captain) of his own ship. By the time he was done about a decade later, he had not only accumulated a great deal of money, but he had also seen much of the known world, starting with the West Indies, Europe, and Africa.

Having quite successfully scratched that career itch, he decided to head back home to be with family. As his brother was already established in Portsmouth, New Hampshire, Whipple settled there, where he went into the mercantile business with his sibling.

In 1767 he married Catherine Moffatt and moved into her family home. As it was also in the town of Portsmouth, Whipple did not have far to resettle into his newly married life.

As a former "citizen of the world," **Whipple** had formed some very strong opinions regarding both totalitarian governments and the will of the people. For that reason and others, he decided to enter politics at the local level.

By 1775 he found himself being elected to represent Portsmouth at the Provincial Congress. The very next year, New Hampshire voted to dissolve the royal government and replace it with their version of a House of Representatives and an Executive Council. **Whipple** played a prominent role in that political transformation.

As such, by the early part of 1776, **Whipple** was elected to the Second Continental Congress. In that body, he quite naturally served on both the Maritime and Commerce Committees.

During the late summer, he proudly signed the **Declaration of Independence**.

That said, signing a document viewed by the Crown as a personal death warrant was not nearly thrilling enough for a man who had spent over fifteen years on one exciting adventure after another around the world. Because of that, he also felt a responsibility to be a part of the New Hampshire Militia, a militia he would soon command as a brigadier general.

And as that then military man, **Whipple** took a very dim view of his fellow colonists who remained loyal to the Crown. So much so, that whenever possible, he felt their treasonous behavior should be met with severe punishment. With that tough-minded mindset, General Whipple went on to command troops at both Saratoga and in the Rhode Island campaign.

After the end of the Revolutionary War, he returned home to serve as both a state legislator and an associate justice of the Superior Court of New Hampshire.

It was believed that **William Whipple** suffered from a heart ailment and that while riding his horse in November **1785** he suffered a heart attack and passed away where he fell. He was fifty-five years of age.

Chapter Fifty-Three

Robert Treat Paine

𝕴 magine being the prosecutor trying to get a conviction of the British officers responsible for the 𝕭𝖔𝖘𝖙𝖔𝖓 𝕸𝖆𝖘𝖘𝖆𝖈𝖗𝖊, and you look across the aisle to find that 𝕵𝖔𝖍𝖓 𝕬𝖉𝖆𝖒𝖘 is defending those men.

That had to take a moment or two to process.

Okay. So, the Dorchester Rat in me is happy to note that we are once again focusing on another Boston guy. Have I mentioned that Boston was known as the "Cradle of Liberty?"

𝕽𝖔𝖇𝖊𝖗𝖙 𝕿𝖗𝖊𝖆𝖙 𝕻𝖆𝖎𝖓𝖊 was born in Boston, Massachusetts, on 𝕸𝖆𝖗𝖈𝖍 𝟏𝟏, 𝟏𝟕𝟑𝟏. As his father had been a minister, it was expected that young Robert would follow in his footsteps. After graduating from Harvard, 𝕻𝖆𝖎𝖓𝖊 did, in fact, give the clergy a good, old-fashioned try. It turned out that he hated it. More than that, he decided to drop out of Boston life—and family pressure—for a bit by becoming, of all things, a merchant marine.

As he had always been a bit weak and frail as a young man, the last thing his family and friends expected of him was for young **Paine** to choose to go to sea for a few years. But choose so he did.

Upon his return to Boston, he was in fact, a bit tougher and mentally stronger, and he had a real edge to him. He decided that a career in law would be best for him. Not only was he admitted to the Massachusetts bar in 1757, but he soon met and married Sally Cobb.

As fate would have it, because of his decision to enter the world of law, he would become involved in the most famous and controversial legal case in Boston History. That, of course, being the **Boston Massacre** trial.

On **March 5, 1770**, five Bostonians were cut down by British redcoat fire. On **October 17, 1770**, the fate of those soldiers was about to be announced in the Boston courtroom. Captain Thomas Preston had claimed they had fired only in self-defense out of fear for their lives. In the corner with him and his men as their defense attorney stood none other than Founding Father and signer of the **Declaration, John Adams**.

In the other corner, looking to get a conviction so Preston and his men could be hanged as soon as possible to appease the mobs of Bostonians gathered outside of the courtroom, was fellow **Founding Father** and **Declaration** signer, **Robert Treat Paine**.

As mentioned earlier, **Adams** prevailed. As to why that was so important, we have the words of **Adams** himself. He described his role in the trial as:

> The greatest service I ever rendered my country. Why? In a town where British soldiers were hated, there had been a fair trial by a jury. In a land where mobs could sway events, the

world saw that justice and liberty were valued as the legal rights of all.[45]

While Paine did lose the case to Adams, his stature among Bostonians went up immeasurably. Not only was he the guy seemingly trying to get the British "murderers" hanged, but he also strongly argued against Parliament's right to house British troops in Boston.

For those reasons and more, he was elected to the First Continental Congress in 1774, where he served ably on several committees. In 1775—July 5 to be precise—things got a bit sticky for him as, once again, he found himself in opposition to highly respected—and powerful—John Adams. That was when certain delegates—Robert Treat Paine near the top of the list, as he had helped to draft it—offered up what would turn out to be the humiliating "Olive Branch Petition" to King George III.

Adams, among other delegates, not only strongly objected to the petition—and may have later leaked a letter to help kill it in London—but to its closing words that quite embarrassingly fawned over and prostrated before the king by saying that the delegates hoped:

> That your Majesty may enjoy a long and prosperous reign, and that your descendants may govern your Dominions with honour to themselves and happiness to their subjects, is our sincere prayer.[46]

Wow. Had the king been before them, it would not have been surprising to see some of those same delegates offer him flowers and candy before attempting to kiss his royal backside.

Instead of giving the back of his hand to the face of those delegates by refusing to even read the petition—as he did— imagine what would have happened to the colonies had the king "agreed" to the terms, knowing so many colonial leaders would do just about anything to avoid a fight for their Liberty.

In this particular case, we should all be grateful that Robert Treat Paine lost again to the wisdom of John Adams.

Or for that matter, for the truly brilliant and Patriotic Abigail Adams, who, upon hearing of the humiliating rejection of the petition by the king, wrote to her husband, John:

> Let us separate, they are unworthy to be our Brethren. Let us renounce them and instead of supplications as formerly for their prosperity and happiness, let us beseech the Almighty to blast their councils and bring Nought to all their devices.[47]

Solid.

Had Abigail Adams been in charge of the Continental Army, the British might have surrendered immediately out of fear of her inexorable strength and resolve.

Going back to Paine, in 1775 he was also elected to the Second Continental Congress. To be sure, he was a committed Patriot who did finally see the wisdom of a clean and complete break from the Crown. That said, in many instances during that Second Congress, he continually managed to get on the nerves of his fellow delegates by objecting to various measures while offering none of his own.

To that very point, his fellow delegates openly called him the "objection maker." As **Benjamin Rush** said, "He seldom proposed anything, but opposed every measure that was proposed by other people..."[48]

After distinguishing himself by voting for and signing the **Declaration of Independence, Paine** went on to be elected as the attorney general of Massachusetts in 1777.

Along with a passion for the law and objecting to the ideas of others, **Paine** had always held a life-long interest in science and became one of the founders of the American Academy of Arts and Sciences in 1780.

In 1783, then-Governor **John Hancock** offered Paine an appointment to the bench of the state Supreme Court. While **Paine** declined that offer, in 1796 when it was offered again, he accepted and served for fourteen years.

Robert Treat Paine passed away in Boston in 1814 at eighty-three years of age.

Chapter Fifty-Four

Elbridge Gerry

kay. Now we come to a truly distinguished Founding Father whose remarkable background includes helping to save Bostonians from starvation after the British Parliament vengefully tried to choke the life out of the city with a blockade, signing the **Declaration of Independence**, being a two-term governor of Massachusetts, and serving as vice president of the United States.

And yet, with all of that stated, many people still only associate his last name with a highly negative political description—one still in use today.

Elbridge Gerry was born in Marblehead, Massachusetts, on **July 17, 1744**.

As a quick aside on the name of "Marblehead," when opposing sports teams come into Boston, the fans will often heckle the best player on that team by screaming: "*Yo,*_____. *We named a town after you. It's called Maaahhblehead.*"

Now, back to **Gerry**. He turned out to be an exceptionally bright young man. So bright in fact, that he entered Harvard at about fourteen years of age and then got his master's degree with a thesis arguing that the colonists should reject the just instituted Stamp Act of 1765. Talk about foresight and courage.

After graduation, Gerry returned home to Marblehead to work in his family's mercantile business. Sometime around 1772, he met Samuel Adams, who further inflamed his already strong anti-Crown feelings.

In 1774 when the British Parliament did shut down Boston Harbor in retaliation for the Boston Tea Party, thirty-year-old Gerry went into action by helping to coordinate and direct the shipments of food and supplies—donated by colonists outraged by the Crown's cruelty—into the harbor of Marblehead.

About one year later—with his name now well-known to the British as an "enemy to the Crown"—Gerry was attending what was surely a Sons of Liberty meeting just outside Boston. After the meeting, he and two others went to sleep in a local tavern in the town.

As it turned out, that night was April 18, 1775. The very night the British redcoats were marching on Lexington and Concord. Gerry and his friends awakened just in time to see the British troops approaching the tavern. Just before the troops kicked in the front door to search it, Gerry and his friends dashed out the back door to safety in the surrounding woods.

Entirely because of his dedicated and courageous opposition to the Crown, Gerry was elected to the Continental Congress in 1776. Not surprisingly, within the congress, he was noted for being one of the loudest voices calling for independence. And in the fall of that year, he signed the Declaration of Independence.

Just about ten years later—and late in life for sure—Gerry met and married Ann Thompson. While he may have been late to marriage, he and Ann still found the time to produce ten children.

Because he was justifiably a hero to the people of Massachusetts, they elected him twice to be their governor, starting in 1810.

As governor—and in the interest of looking out for his party—Gerry was in favor of a redistricting measure that would assist in keeping his party in power. Because of that, the angry opposition almost instantly coined the term "gerrymandering" to describe an act that they felt was unfair to the election process. The term, and its negative connotation, survives to this day.

By 1813 Gerry became President James Madison's vice president. Gerry's was truly a remarkable career.

Elbridge Gerry passed away while vice president in 1814 at seventy years of age. He is the only signer buried in Washington, D.C.

CHAPTER FIFTY-FIVE

Stephen Hopkins

Even if age truly is "only a number," 𝔖𝔱𝔢𝔭𝔥𝔢𝔫 𝔥𝔬𝔭𝔨𝔦𝔫𝔰 holds the record for being the second-oldest signer after Benjamin Franklin. And while he had nothing to do with that bit of fate, he had everything to do with being an incredibly accomplished leader of the Revolution.

𝔥𝔬𝔭𝔨𝔦𝔫𝔰 was born in then-Scituate, Rhode Island, on 𝔐𝔞𝔯𝔠𝔥 7, 1707. While his family was relatively poor and needed him to work the farm, young Hopkins had an unquenchable thirst for knowledge. As such, in the precious minutes allowed to him each day to relax, he used them to educate himself in as many subjects as possible.

Again, a recurring theme for a number of these inspirational 𝔉𝔬𝔲𝔫𝔡𝔦𝔫𝔤 𝔉𝔞𝔱𝔥𝔢𝔯𝔰.

While many thought he was destined to remain a farmer, 𝔥𝔬𝔭𝔨𝔦𝔫𝔰 had other ideas and tried his hand at surveying, the mercantile business, and even shipbuilding.

At around twenty years of age, he met and married Sarah Scott. They would go on to have at least seven children.

By 1732, Hopkins was chosen to be a representative for Scituate in the General Assembly and then served in that body for a number of years.

In some ways more importantly, in 1754 he was chosen as a delegate to the Colonial Convention being held in Albany, New York. It was there that he met and became a great friend of...Benjamin Franklin.

Hopkins and Franklin not only saw eye to eye on almost everything but also discussed the power of the written word in getting out the message for the need for complete independence from the autocratic Crown. Hopkins not only deeply believed in that strategy, but he also put his money and his energy where his mouth was by becoming one of the founders of the *Providence Gazette and Country Journal*, a publication that continually spoke out against the tyrannical acts of the Crown.

Not satisfied with that, in 1764 Hopkins himself authored a paper titled "The Rights of Colonies Examined." In that paper, Hopkins courageously argued against the right of the British Parliament to tax the colonists. More than that, he argued they really could not do anything without the *consent* of the American people. That paper, his words, and his very name soon spread like a beacon of hope across the colonies.

In 1774 this highly intelligent, self-educated, and deeply principled man was elected to the First Continental Congress. Once there, he was not shy about vocalizing his belief that the colonies would have to fight for their liberty. Said Hopkins in part:

> Powder and ball will decide the question. The gun and the bayonet alone will finish the contest in which we are engaged, and any

of you who cannot bring your minds to this mode of adjusting the question had better retire in time.[49]

Incredibly strong and even controversial words to be sure, but words and a mindset that would be proven accurate a few years later.

By 1776, Hopkins was serving in the Second Continental Congress, and when the day finally arrived for him to sign the Declaration of Independence, his hand was shaking from the "palsy" afflicting his body. As he proudly signed, Hopkins declared to all: *"My hand trembles, but my heart does not."*

It was a hand that also helped to draft the Articles of Confederation.

In 1778, he left the Continental Congress to return to Rhode Island to serve in its legislature.

Stephen Hopkins passed away in Providence in 1785 at seventy-eight years of age.

Chapter Fifty-Six

William Ellery

$\mathfrak{S}$ ticking with the theme that age is just a number, we come to the second gentleman from Rhode Island—a man who would become the second-longest-lived signer of the Declaration of Independence.

William Ellery was born in Newport, Rhode Island, on December 22, 1727. His well-to-do father put a premium on education and sent him off to Harvard College. Soon after graduation, William married Ann Remington.

His dream while in college had been to become a lawyer. However, soon after marriage, the children started arriving, and Ellery needed immediate income to help support his rapidly growing family. For that reason, he put off his dream career to enter the mercantile business, a field he would remain in for the next two decades. Ann died in 1764 after fourteen years of marriage and seven children. In 1767 Ellery married Abigail Cary.

Finally, around 1770, with now about sixteen children between two wives, Ellery set aside enough money to pursue his dream job of becoming an attorney. He soon accomplished this goal.

Sometime after becoming an attorney, **Ellery** began paying more and more attention to the interactions between the colonies and the Crown. And the more he did, the angrier he became at what he was witnessing. The treatment of the people of Boston at the hands of the Crown particularly incensed him.

While some records indicate that **William Ellery** was only about five feet tall and a bit on the portly side, he became the personification of the Mark Twain quote: *"It's not the size of the dog in the fight, but the size of the fight in the dog."*

By day, he was a hard-working attorney looking to help his friends and neighbors while seeking to support his family. But at night, he became one of Rhode Island's **Sons of Liberty**, looking to antagonize and subvert the representatives of the Crown in any way possible.

By 1776 **Ellery** was sent to the Second Continental Congress to replace **Samuel Ward**, who had passed away from smallpox. **Ellery** took to the committee assignments like a fish to water. He especially excelled in commercial affairs, foreign relations, and maritime issues.

On **August 2, 1776**, **Ellery** signed the **Declaration of Independence**. It has been reported that, on that day, he stood next to the table to *watch* each of his fellow delegates present sign the birth announcement of our nation. After he did, **Ellery** mentioned to all who would listen at how proud he was to record the look of *"undaunted resolution"*[50] in every single face.

That said, as proud as he rightly was, **Ellery** was also aware that from the second he himself signed that document, he became a man marked for retribution by the Crown. A Crown that exacted its revenge come December of that year when, after seizing Newport, the British Army deliberately sought out Ellery's home to burn to the ground while destroying all around it.

In 1785, Ellery was asked to serve as the chief justice of the Rhode Island Supreme Court. Ellery declined the honor to remain in service to the Continental Congress.

During that same year, William Ellery became one of the loudest and most persistent voices in the nation, condemning slavery in the strongest possible terms while calling for its abolition.

He passed away at his home in Newport, Rhode Island, in 1820 at ninety-two years of age. He was the second-longest-lived signer, after Charles Carroll.

Chapter Fifty-Seven

Samuel Huntington

One day, you are the king's attorney doing the bidding of the Crown within your colony. The next, you have quit your position in shame to join the 𝔖ons of 𝔏iberty in their fight against tyranny.

What would cause a man to make such a drastic decision and put his very life at risk? How about awareness, honor, courage, duty, and sacrifice?

𝔖amuel 𝔥untington was born on 𝔍uly 3, 1731, on a modest farm in Windham, Connecticut. As with a few other signers, his family was not wealthy and needed him to work the farm to help support them all.

𝔖amuel was happy to do so but also wanted more out of life. While he considered the life of a farmer to be not only noble but also a profession essential to the future of his colony, he also had a keen interest in the law. As such, he also began to educate himself during each spare minute he could find during the endless days of hard work.

By his early twenties, he attained his lofty goal by passing the bar and being made an attorney—one who was entirely self-educated with the benefit of borrowed books. Once a lawyer, he moved to the town of Norwich, Connecticut, to set up practice. It was there that he met and married Martha Devotion, a woman whose last name was certainly apt considering her father was a minister.

Soon after that, he was appointed the king's attorney for the town. While acting in that capacity, he also took on a number of other responsibilities and duties. In 1773, Huntington was appointed to the Superior Court of Connecticut. Up until that moment, he had been considered a moderate by most who knew him and someone who sided with the Crown by those who did not.

By 1774, all that began to change. With each passing day, Huntington knew he could no longer ignore or excuse the growing and often cruel abuses of the Crown. It was a time for choosing.

Samuel Huntington chose the liberty of the colonies over his allegiance to the Crown. And when he flipped, he did so in the most dramatic and statement-making way possible. He joined the Sons of Liberty and became a *very* active member.

But again. That was by night.

By day, he walked the path of legislative action.

In 1776, he was not only elected to the upper house of Connecticut's General Assembly but also to the Second Continental Congress. On July 2 of that year, he voted for the Declaration of Independence and signed it shortly thereafter.

Huntington not only served multiple years in that Congress but was also its president when the Articles of Confederation were adopted.

By 1784, he was called home after he was elected as the lieutenant governor of his state. Interestingly, serving in that office at that time also meant that you would be given the duties of the chief judge of the Superior Court.

Two years later, Samuel Huntington was elected governor, one who was beloved by the people of Connecticut. So much so, they kept him in that job until he passed away in 1796 at sixty-five years of age. But before his death, this self-educated and self-made man earned honorary degrees from Yale, Princeton, and Dartmouth.

CHAPTER FIFTY-EIGHT

William Williams

Hopefully over the years, most of us have considered ourselves dedicated and responsible employees trying to carve out a career. Now, imagine one person doing so with one job for over forty years, another for almost thirty years, and the last for forty years. And all of them at *the same time*.

William Williams was born in Lebanon, Connecticut, on April 23, 1731. His father had been a minister for decades and his grandfather one for over five decades. Doing a job well and for decades at a time seemed to be in his blood.

When he was about fifteen, his father sent William off to Harvard. Upon his graduation, he returned home to begin the study of the ministry under the watchful and wise eyes of his father.

Then, one of those life-altering moments happened to William. The French and Indian War was in full swing, and in 1754 he decided to accompany his relative, Colonel Ephraim Williams, on an expedition to Lake George. Sadly, the colonel was soon killed in battle, and as young William tried to process that, he came to learn how the British military looked down their noses at the colonists and considered them nothing more than "common trash."

Once safely back home in Lebanon, William's mind was filled with conflicting and confusing thoughts. The first conclusion he came to was that he no longer wanted to be a member of the clergy.

He decided that the best course of action for him at that point was to enter the mercantile business. But as he began to succeed at that, he felt a calling to serve the people of his area. That decided, he accepted the position of town clerk—a job he would hold for the next forty-four years. Before and during that time, he was also elected as a selectman for his town—a job he performed for over twenty-five years. On top of that, he served in the provincial and then state legislature for about forty years, including as the speaker of the house.

While Williams was one of the most dedicated and responsible workers of his time, he decided he did not want to be married to his jobs. He wanted a wife and children as well. And he got them. At about forty years of age, he married Mary Trumbull—the daughter of the state's future first governor—and together the couple had three children.

In June of 1776, Oliver Wolcott—more on him next—had to leave the Continental Congress due to a brief illness, and Williams was picked to replace him. As Williams did not arrive in Philadelphia until the end of July, he did not get to vote for independence. However, just a few short days later, he had the high honor to sign the Declaration of Independence on behalf of the people of Connecticut.

While at the congress, he also worked on the committee entrusted with framing the Articles of Confederation. In 1788 he attended the convention in Hartford, where Connecticut ratified the US Constitution.

William Williams passed away on **August 2, 1811**—thirty-five years to the day after he signed the **Declaration**. He was eighty years of age.

CHAPTER FIFTY-NINE

Oliver Wolcott

W aste not. Want not. Win a battle.

One of the most reliable bits of incredible trivia from the Revolutionary War entails the toppling of a statue of the hated King George III by—most likely—a band of the **Sons of Liberty** wandering the streets of New York City right after **General George Washington** ordered a reading of the **Declaration of Independence**. Said statue was then collected off the street, cut up, and melted down to make over 42,000 musket balls to fire against the British Army in the winning Battle of Saratoga.

Who could have possibly been responsible for organizing that bit of literally "in your face" Karma?

Oliver Wolcott was born on **November 20, 1726**, in Windsor, Connecticut. He was the youngest of fourteen children. It can certainly be said that young **Oliver** was born into a version of Connecticut "royalty." His father, Roger, was one of the first governors of that colony and, as his child, Oliver led a pampered childhood.

Once old enough, **Oliver** was sent off to Yale, where he distinguished himself in the study of law. However, before graduating, he was asked by the governor of New York—a friend of his father—to assist in raising a militia to help the British forces involved in the French and Indian War.

Young Oliver not only did that, but once done, he went back to Yale to finish his studies and graduate. After graduation, he went right back to the militia he helped to create to serve as a captain in battle against the French.

After that war was over, he returned home with the idea of studying medicine under the supervision of his brother. But before he could get too far down that track, in 1751 he was appointed as the sheriff of New Litchfield County, a position he would hold for the next two decades. It should be noted that while doing that, he also served in the colonial legislature and was a county judge.

Toward the end of January 1755, he married Laura Collins. Together, they would have five children—one of whom would also carve out a place in history.

All the while he was working and raising a family, Wolcott remained in the militia. By 1774 he had risen to the rank of colonel.

In the fall of 1775, he was elected to the Second Continental Congress. While he endeavored to attend as many meetings as possible, much of his time was taken up leading the Connecticut Militia into various battles against the British. During the course of the war, Wolcott commanded fourteen regiments and was made a brigadier general in 1777.

He and his militia defended Long Island, turned back Loyalist raids along the Connecticut coast, and helped to win the crucial Battle of Saratoga. That is the battle in which *his militia* used the 42,000 musket balls he and his family personally melted down from that statue of King George III to use as ammunition. As said before, this Wolcott guy was a certified badass. But even the toughest of people can get sick from time to time. And that is precisely what happened to Wolcott right before the vote for independence. And while he did miss that vote, he was able to come back in October 1776 to sign the Declaration of Independence.

In 1778, while between battles, he was once again elected to the Continental Congress, where he served until 1784.

Two years later, he was elected as the lieutenant governor of the State of Connecticut, a position he held for a decade. In 1787, Wolcott became a member of the state convention that ratified the US Constitution.

In 1796, he was made governor of Connecticut when fellow Declaration signer Samuel Huntington suddenly died in office. Oliver Wolcott himself would then pass away while serving in that role on December 1, 1797. He was seventy-one years of age.

His son, Oliver Wolcott Jr., would go on to serve as the secretary of the Treasury in the administrations of George Washington and John Adams before himself becoming governor of Connecticut.

Chapter Sixty

Matthew Thornton

𝕬 tall, powerful, yet quiet and dignified physician offered up a blueprint for independence before speaking some of the most powerful and inspiring words of the Revolution.

𝔐𝔞𝔱𝔱𝔥𝔢𝔴 𝔗𝔥𝔬𝔯𝔫𝔱𝔬𝔫 was born in Lisburn, County Antrim, Ireland, on 𝔐𝔞𝔯𝔠𝔥 3, 1714. His family immigrated to America when he was about three years of age, settling in what is now the vicinity of Maine.

When young 𝔐𝔞𝔱𝔱𝔥𝔢𝔴 was about eight years of age, Native Americans (Indians) attacked the settlement where his family lived, forcing his mother and father to grab him and flee for their lives as their home went up in flames.

After their escape, they settled in the Worcester area of Massachusetts. After the family reestablished themselves in a new community, young 𝔐𝔞𝔱𝔱𝔥𝔢𝔴 went to local school and excelled at a classical education.

After leaving school, he decided he had a strong interest in medicine and was able to apprentice with a well-known and respected physician in the area. Around 1740, at the age of twenty-six, 𝔗𝔥𝔬𝔯𝔫𝔱𝔬𝔫 established what became a very successful medical and surgical practice in the town of Londonderry, New Hampshire.

Because of his skills as a surgeon, five years later he found himself serving in the New Hampshire Militia during the time of "King George's War" (1745–48). This militia became part of the British forces that captured Louisbourg, the well-known French fortress in Nova Scotia.

After returning to Londonderry, **Thornton** resumed his growing medical practice. About that same time—and after his war experience—he also decided that he needed to get more involved in the politics that was determining his and his neighbors' fate.

Toward that end, in 1758 he was elected to the colonial assembly, where his voice took on more and more prominence. Approximately two years later—at about forty-six years of age—**Thornton** met and married a young woman by the name of Hannah Jack. They would go on to have five children together.

Then came—as it always did—1765 and that incendiary Stamp Act. Even though **Thornton** was by then a colonel serving in the militia under the royal governor, he proceeded to publicly speak out against the act and the oppressive Crown in the strongest terms possible. His words began to alienate the royal governor, just as much as they began to endear **Thornton** to the people of his area and colony. By 1775 he had had enough and drew an uncrossable line when he denounced the "unconstitutional and tyrannical acts of the British Parliament."

After the royal governor realized the mood of the people was tilting dramatically against the Crown—and himself—he fled the colony on a British ship. Soon after he did, **Thornton** was elected president of the New Hampshire Provincial

Congress. Upon assuming that office, the tall, quiet, but highly principled doctor spoke these inspiring and prophetic words:

> Friends and brethren, you must all be sensible that the affairs of America have, at length, come to a very affecting and alarming crisis. The horrors and distresses of a civil war, which till of late, we only had in contemplation, we now find ourselves obliged to realize. Painful beyond expression, have been those scenes of blood and devastation which the barbarous cruelty of British troops have placed before our eyes. Duty to God, to ourselves, to posterity, ends forced by the cries of slaughtered innocents, have urged us to take up arms in our own defense.[51]

After those stirring words, Dr. Thornton became president of the five-man committee that drafted the state constitution. It was adopted on January 5, 1776, making New Hampshire the *first* of the thirteen colonies to establish a constitution.

In September of that year, he was chosen to be a delegate to the Continental Congress. Although he did not take his seat until November 4, 1776, he was still permitted—and highly encouraged—to sign the Declaration of Independence.

Although having no formal legal education, Dr. Thornton was named as a chief justice of the Court of Common Pleas for the Superior Court of New Hampshire, a position he filled until 1782.

Two years later at about seventy-one years of age, he began to serve in the New Hampshire State Senate until 1786. After leaving public life, Dr. Thornton retired to a small farm on the banks of the Merrimac River outside the town of Exeter.

Matthew Thornton passed away while on a visit to his daughter's home in Newburyport, Massachusetts, on June 24, 1803. He was eighty-nine years of age.

CHAPTER SIXTY-ONE

Quotes by the Signers to Live, Fight, and Survive By

Richard Henry Lee: "*That these united colonies are, and of right, ought to be, free and independent states; and that all political connections between them and the state of Great Britain is, and ought to be, totally dissolved.*"

Thomas Jefferson: "*I have sworn upon the altar of God, eternal hostility against every form of tyranny over the mind of man.*"

John Hancock: "*Some boast of being friends to government; I am a friend to righteous government, to a government founded upon the principles of reason and justice; but I glory in publicly avowing my eternal enmity to tyranny.*"

Benjamin Franklin: "*They that can give up essential Liberty to obtain a little temporary safety deserve neither their Liberty nor safety.*"

John Adams: *"Liberty cannot be preserved without a general knowledge among the people, who have a right...and a desire to know; but besides this, they have a right, an indisputable, unalienable, indefeasible, divine right to that most dreaded and envied kind of knowledge, I mean of the characters and conduct of their rulers."*

Roger Sherman: *"The only real security that you can have for all your important rights must be in the nature of your government. If you suffer any man to govern you who is not strongly interested in supporting your privileges, you will certainly lose them."*

Samuel Adams: *"The Sons of Liberty, on the 14th of August, 1765, a Day which ought to be forever remembered in America, animated with a zeal for their country then upon the brink of destruction, and resolved, at once to save her."*

William Hooper: *"Britain has lost us by a series of impolitic, wicked and savage actions as have disgraced a nation of Hottentots. Human patience can bear no more and all ranks people cry, that the cup of bitterness is full running over."*

Joseph Hewes: *"I am anxious to know how they go on in forming a Constitution, and more anxious to know how they defend their Country, for I expect a formal attack has been made on it before this day."*

Charles Carroll: *"Where Liberty will maintain her empire, till a dissoluteness of morals, luxury and venality shall have prepared the degenerate sons of some future age, to prefer their own mean lucre, ye bribes, and the smiles of corruption and arbitrary ministers, to Patriotism, to Glory, and to ye public weal."*

Benjamin Rush: *"Temperate, sincere, and intelligent inquiry and discussion are only to be dreaded by the advocates of error. The Truth need not fear them."*

John Morton: *"They will live to see the hour when they shall acknowledge that it [signing the Declaration of Independence] to have been the most glorious service that I ever rendered my country."*

George Clymer: *"A Printer publishes a lie for which he ought to stand in the pillory, for the people believe in and act upon it."*

James Smith: *"Public officials may have to live in a splendor unsuited to new republics groaning under financial burdens; private individuals fleeing from the tyranny of old governments are in a different position, however."*

James Wilson: *"The executive power is better to be trusted when it has no screen. Sir, we have a responsibility in the person of our President; he cannot act improperly, and hide either his negligence or inattention; he cannot roll upon any other person the weight of his criminality…far from being above the laws he is amenable to them in his private character as a citizen, and in his public character by impeachment."*

Caesar Rodney: *"That it is our fixed, determined and unalterable resolution, by all lawful ways and means in our power, to maintain, defend and preserve our before mentioned rights and liberties, and that we will transmit them entire and inviolate to our posterity."*

John Witherspoon: *"It is only the fear of God that can deliver us from the fear of Man."*

William Whipple: *"Nothing less than the fate of America depends on the virtue of her sons, and if they do not have virtue enough to support the most Glorious Cause ever human beings were engaged in, they don't deserve the blessings of freedom."*

Elbridge Gerry: *"It must be admitted, that a free people are the proper guardians of their rights and liberties."*

Stephen Hopkins: *"Powder and ball will decide the question. The gun and the bayonet alone will finish the contest in which we are engaged, and any of you who cannot bring your minds to this mode of adjusting the question had better retire in time."*

Matthew Thornton: *"Painful beyond expression, have been those scenes of blood and devastation which the barbarous cruelty of British troops have placed before our eyes. Duty to God, to ourselves, to posterity, ends forced by the cries of slaughtered innocents, have urged us to take up arms in our own defense."*

AFTERWORD

Will the Sons and Daughters of Liberty Rise Anew?

For tens of millions of Americans—and millions more around the world—the **56 Signers**—*Plus One*—featured in this book, as well as every one of the other Founding Fathers, did, in fact, create the greatest nation the world has ever known.

A nation that—very much like the Roman Empire—is in the final throes of national suicide because of a totalitarian rule and greed that has abandoned each and every principle our **Founding Fathers** held dear.

As **The 56** knew well: the rule of law matters, a strong military matters, sovereign and protected borders matter, hard work matters, personal accountability matters, rewarding the "best and the brightest" matters, smaller and less intrusive government matters, and faith matters.

Thomas Jefferson often brilliantly articulated the deepest of truths. Two that speak to the message of this book are these:

The God who gave us life, gave us Liberty at the same time.

—*Summary View of the Rights of British America*, **1774**

And, in a letter to 𝕽𝖎𝖈𝖍𝖆𝖗𝖉 𝕳𝖊𝖓𝖗𝖞 𝕷𝖊𝖊 some fifty years later:

Men by their constitutions are naturally divided into two parties: (1) Those who fear and distrust the people and wish to draw all powers from them into the hands of the higher classes. (2) Those who identify with the people, have confidence in them, cherish and consider them as the most honest and safe…. In every country these two parties exist; and in every one where they are free to think, speak, and write, they will declare themselves.[52]

𝕿𝖍𝖔𝖒𝖆𝖘 𝕵𝖊𝖋𝖋𝖊𝖗𝖘𝖔𝖓 could not be more prescient when it comes to the rapidly failing United States of America in 2022.

Those who do "*fear the people*" have "*declared themselves*" to us and have succeeded in drawing "*all power from them into the hands of the higher classes*."

A "higher classes," where literally some 20,000 of the wealthiest and most powerful people in our nation hold almost complete dominion over the other 350 million.

A "higher classes," which is now continually enacting one draconian dictate after the other to ensure that the people are no longer "*free to think, speak, and write*."

Fortunately, those who still do believe in the vision of our 𝕱𝖔𝖚𝖓𝖉𝖎𝖓𝖌 𝕱𝖆𝖙𝖍𝖊𝖗𝖘 and the Republic they sought to create are not yet vanquished. Again, until those who seek complete totalitarian-groupthink-rule imprison us or take our very lives, they *cannot silence us.*

For the moment, we are still "*free to think, speak, and write.*"

And while the Left and the Far Left do control most of the media, academia, entertainment, science, and medicine, there are still ways to make our voices heard.

As stated at the beginning of this book, the simplest but most sure of ways is to become a 2022 peaceful and law-abiding version of a "𝕾𝖔𝖓 𝖔𝖗 𝕯𝖆𝖚𝖌𝖍𝖙𝖊𝖗 𝖔𝖋 𝕷𝖎𝖇𝖊𝖗𝖙𝖞" and spread the history and vision of our 𝕱𝖔𝖚𝖓𝖉𝖎𝖓𝖌 𝕱𝖆𝖙𝖍𝖊𝖗𝖘...*yourself.*

Speak out. Scream out. Resist.

"𝕿𝖍𝖊 𝕸𝖎𝖉𝖓𝖎𝖌𝖍𝖙 𝕽𝖎𝖉𝖊 𝖔𝖋 𝕻𝖆𝖚𝖑 𝕽𝖊𝖛𝖊𝖗𝖊" is there for all of us to duplicate.

It all starts at the local level because power is often taken and stolen at the local level. It can be taken and stolen by those who *do* despise our 𝕱𝖔𝖚𝖓𝖉𝖎𝖓𝖌 𝕱𝖆𝖙𝖍𝖊𝖗𝖘, who *do* want to tear down their statues, who *do* want to defund and even eliminate the police, who *do* want to declare you an "enemy of the socialist state" if you *dare* to question or resist their failed policies.

Our 𝕱𝖔𝖚𝖓𝖉𝖎𝖓𝖌 𝕱𝖆𝖙𝖍𝖊𝖗𝖘 dealt with such malevolence 250 years ago. Their wisdom, their courage, and their fight were the fuel that powered those long-ago torches of liberty. The light from those torches cut through the darkness of tyranny and exposed the lies, the dangers, the ruin, and the pure evil to the suffering people of the colonies.

This illumination united the masses being oppressed, subjugated, imprisoned, and even killed by the tiny minority of "higher classes" seeking to "draw all power" from them.

Because of The 56 and all our Founding Fathers, the people came to realize that the time had come to stand shoulder-to-shoulder as one to declare to their oppressors: *"It stops now. I will no longer allow you to take my livelihood, deny my rights, rob my children of their future, nor silence my voice. I kneel before God, bow to no tyrant, and stand ready to fight for the liberty which was bestowed upon my birth."*

Tell your children, tell your neighbors, tell your coworkers, and tell your friends of the tales of The 56.

Speak of these men, their vision, their sacrifice, and the Republic they created in your houses of worship, your offices, your school boards, your coffee shops, your VFW and American Legion Posts, the aisles of your super stores, your book clubs, and your bowling leagues. Anywhere where you find a receptive audience of one or more.

Cry out against the tyranny and injustice.

Don't let those who "fear and distrust the people" silence *your* voice.

Since the dawn of recorded time, totalitarian regimes, dictators, and the worst of the "higher classes" have always feared the truth because...*they feared the people*. For they knew if the truth somehow did filter down to the masses, they were doomed.

As I write this, those who fear the truth are tightening their viselike grip around the throat of our nation. They do so to maintain their ill-gotten power while filling their personal coffers. But by doing so, they are also cutting off *all oxygen* to the people and institutions that power our land.

If our Republic soon collapses from this assault, combined with the corrosive bile oozing from the wretched, feeble, sniveling, intellectually deficient despots putting personal power and fortune before national survival—*as it surely will*—all will *still not be lost.*

For within the dust, mangled steel, and rubble of our once-great country will lie our salvation. That being the very blueprint needed to build it anew.

A blueprint envisioned, designed, and implemented by 𝔗𝔥𝔢 56 almost 250 years ago.

A blueprint that will exist as long as we keep it alive within us.

A blueprint for a Republic that *will* rise again.

𝕷ibertu.

ACKNOWLEDGMENTS

First and foremost, my deepest gratitude to Anthony Ziccardi for his belief in me and this project.

I would also like to thank Michael L. Wilson for his wise counsel and support.

Next, my never-ending appreciation to Aleigha Kely, Devon Brown, and the entire team at Post Hill Press for their incredible talent, insight, and dedication.

As always, I'd like to thank my nephew Patrick Ryan Ovide (O-Vee-Dee) – my "Best Friend in the Whole-Wide Universe" – for inspiring me daily.

And finally, I would like to thank my wife Leela June for her constant love, support and belief in me.

ENDNOTES

1 McCarthy, Erin. "Roosevelt's 'The Man in the Arena.'" *Mental Floss* (April 23, 2015; updated April 23, 2020), https://www.mentalfloss.com/article/63389/roosevelts-man-arena

2 "Martin Niemöller: 'First They Came for the Socialists...'" *Holocaust Encyclopedia*, https://encyclopedia.ushmm.org/content/en/article/martin-niemoeller-first-they-came-for-the-socialists

3 Lossing, B.J. "Signers of the Declaration of Independence." Geo. F. Cooledge & Brother (January 1, 1848), https://www.amazon.com/Signers-Declaration-Independence-B-Lossing/dp/B0050QHJ4Y

4 "Obama's 2005 remarks reflect strong stance on controlling immigration." The Associated Press (November 2, 2018), https://apnews.com/article/archive-fact-checking-2477111077

5 Trump, Donald J. *I Am the Winner: A Presidential Autobiography of Donald J. Trump.* Knox Paulson, 156, https://books.google.com/books?id=gAjBDwAAQBAJ&pg=PA156&lpg=PA156&dq=%E2%80%9CI+voted,+when+I+was+a+senator,+to+build+a+barrier+to+try+to+prevent+illegal+immigrants+-from+coming+in.%E2%80%9D&source=bl&ots=Tk4WCoXsZc&sig=ACfU3U0Ve8g_GKxPEhV79IlPlxZFIsjrBg&hl=en&sa=X&ved=2ahUKEwjRjIyv-670AhWXQs0KHcaQDjIQ6AF6BAgCEAM#v=onepage&q=%E2%80%9CI%20voted%2C%20when%20I%20was%20a%20senator%2C%20to%20build%20a%20barrier%20to%20try%20to%20prevent%20illegal%20immigrants%20from%20coming%20in.%E2%8.0%9D&f=false

6   MacKinnon, Douglas. "When Historians Get Hysterical." *New York Post* (January 22, 2019), https://nypost.com/2019/01/11/when-historians-get-hysterical/

7   Rosenbaum, Joseph, "Spielberg's Portrait of Lincoln Is A Bust." *Forward* (November 9, 2012), https://forward.com/culture/165443/spielbergs-portrait-of-lincoln-is-a-bust/

8   Dawn, Randee. "Steven Spielberg Returns Guns to 'E.T.' for 30th Anniversary Release." *NBC News* (May 31, 2012), https://www.nbcnews.com/pop-culture/pop-culture-news/steven-spielberg-returns-guns-e-t-30th-anniversary-release-flna805133,

9   Tullai, Martin. "Lincoln and the Declaration." *The Baltimore Sun* (February 11, 1994), https://www.baltimoresun.com/news/bs-xpm-1994-02-11-1994042079-story.html

10 Lossing, Ibid., https://www.amazon.com/Signers-Declaration-Independence-B-Lossing/dp/B0050QHJ4Y

11 Lee, Richard. "Memoir of the Life of Richard Henry Lee, and His Correspondence with the Most Distinguished Men in America and Europe, Vol. 1 of 2: Illustrative of…of the American Revolution (Classic Reprint)." December 9, 2018, https://www.amazon.com/Memoir-Richard-Correspondence-Distinguished-America/dp/0331634937

12 "Letter from John Adams to Abigail Adams, 3 July 1776, 'Had a Declaration…'" *Massachusetts Historical Society*, https://www.masshist.org/digitaladams/archive/doc?id=L17760703jasecond

13 "Remarks at a Dinner Honoring Nobel Prize Winners of the Western Hemisphere." *American Presidency Project*, (April 29, 1962), https://www.presidency.ucsb.edu/documents/remarks-dinner-honoring-nobel-prize-winners-the-western-hemisphere

14 Library of Congress, Thomas Jefferson Papers 1606 to 1827, https://www.loc.gov/collections/thomas-jefferson-papers/articles-and-essays/the-thomas-jefferson-papers-timeline-1743-to-1827/1774-to-1783/

15 "The History of America's Independence." July 4, 2021. *The Signa*, *https*://signalscv.com/2021/07/the-history-of-americas-independence-day/

16 "Gage, Thomas (1721–1787) Proclamation of Amnesty in Boston to All But Samuel Adams and John Hancock." *The Gilder Lehrman Institute of American History,* https://www.gilderlehrman.org/collection/glc04781

17 Franklin, Benjamin. 1793. *The Private Life of the Late Benjamin Franklin.* London: J. Parsons, https://www.raptisrarebooks.com/product/the-private-life-of-the-late-benjamin-franklin-first-edition/

18 Bartlett, John. *Bartlett's Familiar Quotations: A Collection of Passages, Phrases, and Proverbs Traced to Their Sources in Ancient and Modern Literature (17th Edition).* Little, Brown and Company: November 1, 2002, https://www.amazon.com/Bartletts-Familiar-Quotations-Collection-Literature/dp/0316084603/ref=asc_df_0316084603/?tag=hyprod-20&linkCode=df0&hvadid=312128284741&hvpos=&hvnetw=g&hvrand=145404218 24505696056&hvpone=&hvptwo=&hvqmt=&hvdev=c&hvdvc mdl=&hvlocint=&hvlocphy=9013085&hvtargid=pla-53073863 3024&psc=1

19 Adams, Samuel. 1772. "Samuel Adams Describes the Situation in Massachusetts in 1772." *Digital History,* https://www.digitalhistory.uh.edu/disp_textbook.cfm?smtID=3&psid=144#:~:-text=As%20one%20of%20the%20chief,also%20a%20key%20instigator%20of

20 Adams, Samuel. *The Writings of Samuel Adams 1770–1773.* Palala Press: December 8, 2015, https://www.amazon.com/Writings-Samuel-Adams-1770-1773/dp/1347910840

21 "Colonel Fenton's 'Confidential and Verbal Message' for Samuel Adams." *Boston 1775, August 18, 2018,* https://boston1775.blogspot.com/2018/08/colonel-fentons-confidential-and-verbal.html

22 Lossing, Ibid., https://www.amazon.com/Signers-Declaration-Independence-B-Lossing/dp/B0050QHJ4Y

23 The Inner Temple website, https://www.innertemple.org.uk/who-we-are/history/#:~:text=In%20the%20middle%20of%20the,the%20Temple%20site%20and%20buildings.

24 "Our People Have Fire." *The Baltimore Sun*, July 3, 2017, https://www.baltimoresun.com/opinion/editorial/bs-ed-0704-samuel-chase-20170627-story.html

25 History, Art & Archives, History.House.Gov

26 Maryland State Archives, September 22, 2021, https://msa.maryland.gov./

27 GovInfo website, www.govinfo.gov

28 Henry, Patrick. "Give Me Liberty Or Give Me Death." March 23, 1775. USHistory.org, https://www.ushistory.org/documents/libertydeath.htm

29 Lossing, Ibid., https://www.amazon.com/Signers-Declaration-Independence-B-Lossing/dp/B0050QHJ4Y

30 National Geographic Explorer website, www.nationalgeographic.org

31 USHistory.org website, www.ushistory.org

32 Dr. Benjamin Rush: Our Forgotten Founding Father. November 4, 2018. Robert J. Morgan website, https://www.robertjmorgan.com/uncategorized/dr-benjamin-rush-our-forgotten-founding-father/

33 Lossing, Ibid., https://www.amazon.com/Signers-Declaration-Independence-B-Lossing/dp/B0050QHJ4Y

34 Descendants of the Signers of the Declaration of Independence website, www.dsdi1776.com

35 National Archives website, www.archives.gov

36 Revolutionary Ware and Beyond website,. Revolutionary-war-and-beyond.com.

37 Hunt, William. January 1, 1849. "American Biographical Panorama," https://www.amazon.com/American-Biographical-Panorama-FACSIMILE-William/dp/B007T0H0X4

38 Yale Alumni Magazine website, Yalealumnimagazine.com

39 Constituting America website, Constitutingamerica.org

40 Princeton Alumni Weekly website, www.paw.princeton.edu

41 Struthers, John. 1828. *The History of Scotland, from the Union to the Abolition of the Heritable Jurisdictions in MDCCXLVIII.* Blackie, Fullarton, & Company, https://books.google.com/books?id=rQ1IAAAAMAAJ&pg=PA327&lpg=PA327&dq=

%E2%80%9Cfrom+curiosity+to+see+a+battle%E2%80%9D+
Historic+Scotland&source=bl&ots=hSjDfNfwgY&sig=ACfU
3U0oBeypVwbbO1elU9hUFR3L69lXQw&hl=en&sa=X&ved=
2ahUKEwi0kMz3n6_0AhU5kYkEHVvvCQ4Q6AF6BAg
DEAM#v=onepage&q=%E2%80%9Cfrom%20curiosity%
20to%20see%20a%20battle%E2%80%9D%20Historic%
20Scotland&f=false

42 ReserveBar website, https://www.reservebar.com/products/dram-
buie?utm_source=google&utm_medium=cpc&utm_content=12753
9693971&utm_term=&utm_campaign=%5BG%5D%20Google%20-
%20DSA&gclid=CjwKCAiAv_KMBhAzEiwAs-rX1AwR
nsgDIxFM6rTDP7fi79TuGz1Om0v56XxAAHd3WIAx-
nYl5MQdytBoCPvMQAvD_BwE

43 John Witherspoon biography, Revolutionary War website,
https://www.revolutionary-war.net/john-witherspoon/#:~:text=
In%20answer%20to%20an%20objection,signed%20the%20
Declaration%20of%20Independence.

44 Lossing, B.J. "Signers of the Declaration of Independence." Geo. F.
Cooledge & Brother (January 1, 1848), https://www.amazon.com/
Signers-Declaration-Independence-B-Lossing/dp/B0050QHJ4Y

45 National Park Service website, https://www.nps.gov/bost/learn/
historyculture/massacre-trial.htm

46 History.com website, www.history.com

47 History.com website, "Abigail Adams Leads Rhetorical Charge
Against Britain." November 12, 1775, https://www.history.
com/this-day-in-history/abigail-adams-leads-rhetorical-charge-
against-britain

48 "Delegate Discussions: Benjamin Rush's Characters." Harvard
University Declaration Resources Project, August 26, 2016,,
https://declaration.fas.harvard.edu/blog/dd-rush

49 Constitutingamerica.org, Ibid.

50 "William Ellery," Signers of the Declaration, National Park
Service, https://www.nps.gov/parkhistory/online_books/declara-
tion/bio9.htm

51 Adams, Charles Thornton. *Matthew Thornton of New Hampshire: A Patriot of the American Revolution (Classic Reprint).* Forgotten Books, February 21, 2018, https://www.amazon.com/Matthew-Thornton-New-Hampshire-Revolution/dp/0332032469

52 Bartlett, Ibid., https://www.amazon.com/Bartletts-Familiar-Quotations-Collection-Literature/dp/0316084603/ref=asc_df_0316084603/?tag=hyprod-20&linkCode=df0&hvadid=312128284741&hvpos=&hvnetw=g&hvrand=3346212047940310853&hvpone=&hvptwo=&hvqmt=&hvdev=c&hvdvcmdl=&hvlocint=&hvlocphy=9013085&hvtargid=pla-530738633024&psc=1